Flying in Africa

True Stories

Volume 1

Real life stories inspired by paging through my Logbooks
after a lifetime as a pilot.

by

Jim Davis

Text copyright © 2012 Shelly Kennard Davis
All Rights Reserved

About the Author

Jim Davis was born and educated in Kenya in the 'Out of Africa' days.

He has three passions in life – flying, teaching and writing. And he was lucky enough to combine them all.

Flying led him into many sides of aviation – instructing, charter, aerial-photography, corporate-flying, bush-flying, pylon-racing, aerobatics, sky-writing and service in both the RAF and the South African Air Force.

Teaching, brought him a career as a flying instructor and air-school owner.

And his talent for writing, has neatly tied all three loves together.

Jim claims that he has never worked in his life – he has just had fun. He borrowed money from the bank and bought a derelict WW II RAF base in Port Alfred. Forty-five years of disuse had left the place in a mess. There were no roofs on the buildings and many of walls had been knocked down by folks who wanted the bricks to build their farm houses.

Jim resurrected the buildings and slowly built it into the biggest and most well-respected flying school in Africa: 43 Air School.

Jim is the Author of several books, including PPL – A Practical Book about Flying Safely, and Flight Tests. He has been writing monthly columns for flying magazines in South Africa and Australia since the 1980's. He has over 15,000 flying hours including about 10,000 hours of flying instruction.

Jim Davis is a respected name in aviation in South Africa and Australia. He is now lives, and writes, in the beautiful village of Wilderness, on Africa's south coast.

Foreword

"Just keep reading, all will be explained", Jim texted me when I asked him arbitrary questions like what the heck is a Matchless? And then a few lines later, all is revealed, and my knowledge of motorbikes is expanded.

I find I am feeling tremendously privileged that Jim has asked me to compile his stories for Kindle, because as I sit here, reading through the chapters while waiting for my student to complete his pre-flight before we can go and fly, I am reduced to tears of mirth. His stories are mostly entertaining, sometimes sobering, and his rendition of them is simply masterful.

I am quite sure you will enjoy them just as much as I have.

Telani Lithgow
Senior Flight Instructor & Author of the Lana Aire Flight Training Made Simple series also available on Kindle
www.flight-training-made-simple.com

* * *

In this new series Jim is prompted by his logbooks to tell us stories about fascinating people, amazing flights and the lessons he has learned through his long career in aviation.

My first flying
lesson is not in my logbook
because I was only ten.
Also I didn't really
know
it was
meant
to be a
flying
lesson.
We lived
in Kitale,
a little farming town in the north-west of Kenya.
My hero was Dennis Pharazyn, an instructor who owned a Tiger Moth
My mom worked at the school where Dennis gave evening lectures
on aerodynamics, so it was easy for me to attend.
I sat
in the
front
took
notes
and drew diagrams

Table of Contents

My First Flying Lesson 1
The Royal Air Force 3
Chippie Lunacy 6
MG Lunacy 7
Some Messing Around and a Yellow Cub 10
Cubs and instructors 12
Bossie, Bombdoors & Syd 20
PPL, Placo, Hired and Fired 29
Old Piet, Mr. Piper and Eric 39
Flying with Mr. Piet 47
A Bug in the Cockpit 51
Komatipoort to Stegi 56
The Pay Rise 62
Hypoxia 66
On Fire 70
Hendrik and the Tiger 73
Zingi and the Auster 77
Dendron 81
The Moth and the Milk-Stool 85
Too Stupid to be Scared 89
Bombdoors & Guti 98
Folks Coming Second 106
Neville 115
Scary Stuff Both Ways 125
Windhoek 133

My First Flying Lesson

My first flying lesson is not in my logbook – because I was only ten. Also I didn't really know it was meant to be a flying lesson.

We lived in Kitale, a little farming town in the north-west of Kenya. My hero was Dennis Pharazyn, an instructor who owned a Tiger Moth. My mom worked at the school where Dennis gave evening lectures on aerodynamics, so it was easy for me to attend. I sat at the front, took notes and drew diagrams of Bernoulli's venturi.

At weekends I would borrow my mom's Raleigh bicycle, with a wicker basket on the front, and pedal out to the airfield where I helped with refuelling, pumping tyres and wiping oil from the hangar floors.

Naturally I hoped that someone would offer me a flight, and eventually Dennis did. He helped me into the front seat of his Tiger, strapped me in and explained how to use the Gosport tube for talking to him. It consisted of a dirty-green rubber cup mounted on a flexible metal tube in front of me. If I spoke into this my voice would rattle down the tube which split into two, one for each ear, in his headset – like a doctor's stethoscope.

He had the same in the rear cockpit. Once I had donned the leather helmet, he tested the system by talking to me from his rubber cup. It worked splendidly, apart from making him sound like Donald Duck.

Very soon there where shouts of, "stick back", "throttle set", and eventually, "contact". The whole collection of wires, wood, fabric and Victorian engineering started to rattle and shake as the Gypsy spluttered into life. The aeroplane suddenly became a living thing.

Someone pulled the chocks out, there was a burst of power, a blast of wind from the prop, and we started moving over the rough grass. The aircraft rocked alarmingly and the tail-skid clattered as we zigzagged from side to side, so Dennis could see where we were going.

We lined up on the grass runway. Dennis said: "Are you ready to go?"

"Yes, sir." I yelled into the Gosport.

Dennis took full power and within seconds the skid stopped clattering, the tail came up and I could see where we were going. Moments later the main wheels stopped rumbling and the ground drifted away.

In that instant I knew I would spend the rest of my life flying.

The lesson was very interesting. Dennis, using his Donald Duck voice, said: "Quack quack quackerty quack...quack... quacking quack." Or something. I naturally answered: "Yes, sir."

After that the aircraft wandered around the sky while Dennis did a bit more quacking. Then suddenly he said, quite clearly: "OK I have got her now."

So no one was flying the Tiger, when it was my turn.

Sadly, many years later, Dennis was killed near Howick, in Natal, doing a home-made let-down through the clouds into Pietermaritzburg. In fact the main road to the airport, Pharazyn Way, is named after him.

*   *   *

The Royal Air Force

After school in Kenya, I went to England and joined the RAF at Cranwell. I don't have my first logbook because the swines kept it. However my summary states that I was N2, which means assistant, deputy navigator – under training. The aeroplane was a Vickers Valetta, a piggy-looking, Dak-like thing with two Bristol Hercules engines, each putting out 1975 hp.

Inside, there were six navigators' stations, each with its own Gee set. This was a malevolent device that reminded one of Marconi's first experiments with wireless. You expected it to smell of paraffin, and have a wick underneath. There was a port-hole which allowed you to peer inside and search for faint green blips.

We had to twiddle many knobs in order to derive numerical information from the blips. From this we were meant, in a manner that I never grasped, to identify our position on the surface of the planet.

I was extremely bad at this, and many other tasks - including marching. On one occasion Flight Sergeant Holt, known as bog-brush because of his bristly hair-cut, bellowed at me, from across the parade ground, that I was a Mad Matabele, and on another day, he decided I was a Wild Watusi. Even my mentor, a kindly bloke named Hallows, informed me that I was a great somnolent bugger (I had to look it up in the library).

The weekly Mess-night, when they dug out the silver candle sticks and starched napkins, highlighted another flaw in my upbringing – a lack of etiquette. It seems that her Majesty held no grudge against officers who dropped spoons on the floor, but the picking up of cutlery really got right up her nose.

This crime caused the mess-president to invite the assembled company of about 50 officer-cadets to drinks in the anti-room, at my expense. At the time my monthly salary was £4.17s. 6d (AU$9.80 in real money) so it took me many months to pay off my mess-bill.

Then there was my ineptitude in the classroom - I found Newton's laws boring, irrelevant, and incomprehensible. But perhaps the least understandable duty I faced, as a trainee pilot, was filing a big lump of iron into a perfect one-inch cube, which a man in a brown coat measured with a micrometer.

Finally, my lack of dedication to the task of applying Blanco, Brasso and boot polish, when added to my other imperfections, caused her Majesty to lose it. She invited me to leave the defence of her dominions to other more competent personnel. Well, she didn't actually do this herself, she got Flight Lieutenant Johnstone to inform me.

Surprisingly Flt Lt Johnson told a porky: he wrote in my Certificate of Service that my conduct had been 'exemplary'. How very British. He shoved me into a Vickers Viking and sent me back to Kenya - hoping to never see me again. I was still 17.

In an ironic twist of fate I did indeed return to Cranwell, as something of a VIP, many years later - but I will tell you about that another day.

Pic below: Me in London, Dec 1956, age 17, just before going into the RAF.

* * *

Chippie Lunacy

Here are the first three entries in my next proper logbook. This was at Nairobi's Wilson Airport:

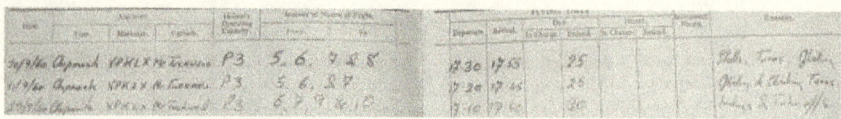

I am appalled by these entries. My very first flying lesson consisted of stalls. And the lesson lasted 25 minutes. At Nairobi's density altitude it would have taken us most of that time to start-up, taxi and climb to 3000 ft AGL.

Even more remarkable, my instructor, Mr. Tuckwell, considered me ready for circuits and bumps after a total of 50 minutes. Actually it's not remarkable, it is plain stupid - trying to teach a pupe to land an aeroplane before he has learned to fly it.

The problem was compounded by the unbelievably short flights in the circuit - between 20 and 35 minutes each. It probably indicated the maximum time Mr. Tuckwell could tolerate my presence. Consequently my landings held much potential for mutilation of both man and machine. They also left my confidence in tatters.

I endured five hours of this before concluding that the RAF had assessed me correctly when they wrote in my Certificate of Service that I was 'Unlikely to make an efficient pilot'.

* * *

MG Lunacy

Before moving on I have to confess to a piece of non-aviation insanity which justifies the RAF's belief that they could get along pretty well without me.

The day before my first Chipmunk flight with Mr. Tuckwell (instructors didn't have first names in those days) happened to be my 21st birthday. It was memorable because I spent much of the day in court defending a string of traffic violations. Here's what happened.

A few weeks earlier my mate, Tom, and I had been loitering along a new multi-lane highway just west of Nairobi city centre. We were in my MG TC from which I had removed not only the windscreen but also the complete exhaust system. Why? Because it made a sound like a racing car. And because I was extremely immature.

We stopped at the side of the road to enjoy a quiet smoke. The lack of a windscreen made smoking difficult while on the trot.

Soon we were joined by a Police Peugeot, and a seven-year-wonder – a much-loathed Brit cop on a seven-year contract. He immediately spotted my lack of windscreen, which was meant to harbour my license and insurance discs (it didn't really matter because they were both expired). After taking my details, and noting the various deficiencies in my car - too much play in the steering, crappy tyres, no brake lights, and so on; he told me to 'move along'.

This presented a new problem. If I started the engine he would immediately hear the missing exhaust and add this to the list of crimes. So I told him that we were out of petrol and a mate had gone to fetch some. He said I should move along as soon as the petrol arrived. And off he drove.

Now, I have no explanation for my next piece of insanity. I simply didn't depart the scene of the crime. So 15 minutes later the rozzer was breathing down my neck again. I explained that my petrol-getter had failed to take a can, and that I had just given him one, and that was him driving away in a yellow VW Beetle that I pointed out. The officer leaped into his Peugeot and set off in pursuit of the innocent Beetle.

Realising that no good could come of this, I did a 180 and put foot into the face of the oncoming traffic, on the wrong side of the freeway.

Unfortunately the custodian of the law was on his toes, he spotted my getaway tactic in his mirror, copied my 180, and gave chase. Now my MG, although tatty, was no slouch and could certainly out-pace a pathetic Peugeot 203. So, after a gangster-style car-chase through the middle of Nairobi, I managed to shake him off.

20 year-olds are not strong on consequences. I was therefore amazed to have the peeler visit me at work the next morning. He had the look of a policeman who was about to avenge the wrongs of the world. He also had a collection of documents listing my crimes. He mentioned in passing that I would spend much of my future in jail. This was a bit of a bummer as I was planning to marry an extremely sexy Scottish red-head.

Anyhow the court date was set for my 21st birthday - 19 September 1960. I couldn't afford a lawyer, so I thought my best defence would be to make the court think they had the wrong guy. They would be expecting an arrogant James Dean character in jeans and a leather jacket, so I decided to be a myopic, bumbling academic.

I borrowed a worn-out black cotton jacket with chalk dust on the shoulders, torn cuffs, and holes in the elbows. I also wore a pair of Coke-bottle glasses, through which I could see almost nothing.

Every time anyone spoke to me I would get a fright and drop my notes, or my pen into the bottom of the witness-box. The court would have to wait as I doubled over to retrieve the lost article. While I scratched around pretending to look for my property, only my bum would be visible to the assembly.

I also made a point of peering myopically at the wrong person whenever anyone spoke to me. I could see my act had taken the prosecutor by surprise. No James Dean - only the village idiot. His Worship was also having trouble linking the alleged wild-west events to this gibbering pillock. Eventually he lost patience and demanded clarification from the prosecuting bobby.

There was a long pause during which absolutely nothing happened. The prosecutor again called for the policeman.

Guess what. The constable wasn't in court, heaven knows why. The result was that I was acquitted, for lack of evidence, and the policemen was fined £20 for contempt of court.

Now back to aviation.

* * *

Some Messing Around and a Yellow Cub

My miserable start, both with her Majesty and Mr. Tuckwell, left me with the belief that I was not cut out for driving aeroplanes. So I again served her Majesty in the capacity of a Customs officer in Mombasa. Then I was a motor mechanic and car salesman in Moshi, at the base of Kilimanjaro, a piece of vertical scenery which I scrambled up - three times. I also indulged in motorcycle track and hill-climb racing, while employed as a coffee farmer at Thika. Then I was a credit controller, a Tyre salesman, and a hangman's assistant in Nairobi. I didn't actually get involved in dangling people. The hangman, Jack Ainsworth, had a sideline - repossessing cars for HP companies. It was to this rather risky pursuit that I was assigned. I say risky because most of Jack's customers were black people who didn't like having their cars taken away by white people. Also the Mau Mau nonsense was going on.

So here's how I got back into aviation. I moved to South Africa where I was employed as the manager of a chicken-farm, at Garsfontein, just south of Pretoria.

One day a Yellow Cub flew over, and I suddenly remembered that I wanted to be a pilot.

Within days I found myself in the back of an identical aeroplane belonging to the Pretoria Flying Club at Wonderboom. The front seat was occupied by a pleasant-natured soul called Buitenhuis. He also had no first name, and his bulk obscured most of the instruments. I think he was a good instructor - certainly a patient one. We flew in the cool calm of the early mornings, and I loved it. Every second of it.

Part of the pre-flight inspection was to grab the wingtip and shake it vigorously up and down. It used to clonk, indicating it was unserviceable, due to elongated bolt holes in the strut mountings. Buitenhuis would just smile gently and carry on as if everything was okay - so I assumed it was.

Sometimes I would fly with 'Dirty' Bosman, who was noticeably unwashed, and had something of an agricultural outlook on life. His favourite saying was, "Don't fokking ask why - just fokking do it!"

During one landing, as we approached the apex of a particularly spectacular bounce, he twisted round in his seat so I could see every crud-filled pore of his face. I watched fascinated as a small stalactite of spit on his top lip blew outwards as he bellowed, "Davis, you are going to crash this fokking aircraft."

"I know, Bossie, I know," was all I could splutter before we sailed into the ground again.

It was on such days that I reflected on the opinions of Her Majesty and Mr. Tuckwell.

* * *

Cubs and instructors

Flying training requires both an aeroplane and an instructor. Let me tell you about the aeroplane first - the little J3 Cub - then I will tell you how I remember some of my early instructors. Actually the stories intertwine - but I will do my best.

As Model T Fords sold in any colour, as long as it was black, so William T Piper's Cubs came in all colours called yellow. They are meant to be flown from green fields peppered with daisies.

As you walk towards the little aeroplane you realise it is about as basic as it could be. The four tiny cylinders poke out of the nose with little black ears to scoop the air round them. The spark plugs and their wires are there in plain sight.

The cowlings seem to be made out of Coke,(soft-drink), can material. They are held on with nappy pins. The tailplane has no shape – it is just a flat thing. The ailerons are worked by exposed wires that run up behind the struts, go around pulleys and are attached to the horns by pins and split-pins. In fact much of the aeroplane depends on bits of bent wire. Hell, even the door handle is a bit of bent wire.

The preflight is so simple it needs no discussion as long as you check about a thousand split pins and nappy pins.

The pilot-in-command, or student, clambers into the back seat and is immersed in a smell of dope, (the glue-like stuff you paint on aircraft fabric to make it tighten up after re-covering the aircraft frame), hot oil and avgas. The instructor, or passenger, has to go through some spine-wrenching contortions to get into the front. As soon as he is comfortable you realise you can't see a damn thing except his back. You have no forward visibility at all, and all the instruments are hidden.

When I say 'all' the instruments, there is a rev-counter which works the wrong way, a one-handed altimeter that only shows thousands of feet, an ASI, (Air Speed Indicator), compass, a ball, and a combined temp and pressure gauge. Oh, and there is another bit of wire, with a cork, to tell you the level of the fuel in the little 45 litre tank behind the panel.

As you strap yourself in, you have to make sure that your seat belt doesn't go round the rudder cables which run along the floor on either side of your seat.

Let's take stock of what you have under your command. No, not the fuel cock that's under the panel, and way beyond your reach. Altimeter setting knob? No - also out of reach. Master switch? There isn't one – no battery to switch on. Lights, radios, starter? Nope – we don't have any of those things. But you can operate the door handle, the rudder pedals and heel brakes, the stick – obviously – the carb-heat, trim and throttle on the left side-wall, and mag switch at the wing root above your left shoulder. That's it.

So when you train in a Cub, at a quiet country strip, the stick and rudder teach you about aerodynamics, the throttle, mags and carb-heat teach you about engine handling, and the trim teaches you to fly with a delicate touch. The door handle is your ventilation control – you can fly with the door open or closed, depending on temperature.

So there are no distractions to take your mind away from pure flying, which means you can go solo in six hours, and learn all you need to be a safe pilot in just 40 hours.

Anyhow here we are strapped in and ready to go. Some guy goes round the front and tells you to stand on the heel brakes, which are minute and awkward as hell. He then calls for you to set the throttle and hold the stick fully back. Finally he yells "Contact" so you switch on the mags and reply "Contact". He swings the prop, and with any luck the whole thing rattles into life.

The tiny engine makes a muted clatter – the same comfortable sound that your granny's Singer sewing machine used to make.

Taxying is demanding – you can see nothing ahead. You open the door and stick your head well out to the right to make sure there is nothing immediately ahead. Once you get going you need serious zig-zags to see what you are about to bump into.

The heel brakes are feeble and difficult to get at. In a crosswind, they will soon cook and fade – so you have to stop and let them cool down. Cubs are made for grass patches – not miles of tarmac.

When you get to the holding point you can try doing a run-up at 2100 rpm, but the brakes won't hold; and you realise you should have done it against the chocks outside the hangar.

For vital actions, you check the controls, set the trim and look for other traffic before lining up.

The handle of the throttle is a red wooden ball. You move it forwards and the 65 horses take the revs to 2300, and the clattering will get a bit louder. She gradually eases into a trot and you can get the tail up and see what lies ahead.

She drifts off the ground at 40 mph. Then you must level the nose immediately and wait for 55 before climbing. The front seat occupant must twist to the right so you can see the ASI.

If you are doing circuits and bumps on the Reef and it is a warmish day, you need to turn crosswind at about 200 ft. 500 ft would take you so far away you might lose the airfield. Before turning you must lower the nose to get to 60 mph. On a cool day, with one up, you might be able to climb as high as 700 ft on downwind.

Here's what the POH says about landing:

1. Push carburettor heat ON prior to throttling back for glide, or for any other flight manoeuvre.
2. Glide between 50-60 MPH depending upon loading of airplane and gust conditions.

NOTE: "Clear" engine by opening throttle gently, every 200-250 feet of descent during a
long glide so that engine temperature will be maintained. Throttle action on the part of the pilot should be smooth and gentle at all times.

The POH is remarkably silent on the subject of the landing – in fact, it says nothing. Bossie was more explicit, "Get the fokking stick in your fokking guts." He was right, of course, but he never told me exactly when to apply this delicate procedure.

Sometimes I would do it too early, which resulted in a balloon. And sometimes I would only do it after the wheels touched, which had much the same result.

(Actually, it's extremely poor instruction - telling a pupe what to do with the stick. Rather tell him what to do with the aeroplane. But it took me some years to find that out.)

The Cub's simple honesty made up for Bossie's lack of instructional finesse.

I remember being trapped in that miserable stage when life consists of endless sessions of circuits and bumps – each seemingly worse than the one before. Rather than tell me what I was doing wrong, and make suggestions as to how I might improve my performance, Bossie would, from the front seat, bellow his opinion of my most recent contact with the planet: "That's the worst fokking landing I have ever seen."

Although probably true, this sort of comment did little to help me rectify the problem.

Being wedged in the front seat, Bossie was obliged to grab one of the diagonal struts behind the windscreen and twist his frame to one side so I could strain my neck the other way and glimpse the airspeed indicator and the never-centred ball.

After 5 hrs and 25 minutes of flying with the Pretoria Flying Club, they told me that my next lesson would be with the CFI - Mike Kemp - "to see if you are any good." And so it was that at 0650 local time, on the morning of the 6th of April 1963, Mike, my first instructor with a Christian name, told me, "Bugger off on your own, and don't bend the aeroplane."

There was a vacuous space in the area normally occupied by my various critics. I could see all the instruments - what a treat. The Cub and I popped into the air in less than the length of a football field and the ground moved away more rapidly than before. I broke into a lusty delivery of, "Oh what a beautiful morning", from Oklahoma. Messrs Rodgers and Hammerstein would have cringed at my rendition.

I continued my vocal onslaught on their ballad throughout the circuit, to the exclusion of any checks that were expected of me. In fact I was still at it during the approach and surprisingly graceful return to earth. It only stopped when I taxied within earshot of the grinning Mike.

Then he disappeared to fly a Dakota for the airline.

When you are not doing circuits in a Cub, the only reason to venture above 500 ft AGL would be to practice stalls, steep turns and spins. If you kick off at Wonderboom (4100 ft), with two up, it takes a long time to put 3000 ft between yourself and the ground.

Steep turns are limited by power. At 3000 ft above the beach you may have enough grunt to sustain a 45 degree banked turn. At 3000 ft above Pretoria, it's not going to happen.

Stalls, as you would expect with that gentle Clark Y wing, are pleasantly straightforward. There is no stall hooter, no light, and no warning shudder. And neither are they needed. The controls get sloppy and she gently stops flying and nods her head.

Spins are a delight, although we sometimes have to use a bit of power to get enough rudder control to make it happen. Then you throttle back as soon as she gets going. She settles into a gentle and predictable spin that you can leave as long as you like. And she recovers the moment you ask her.

As you enter the spin, remember to listen for the clonk that tells you the wings are not properly attached.

But training in a Cub wasn't all golden days and roses. One evening I was boarding my Matchless to go home, when another instructor, Buitenhuis, hailed me and mentioned that on Wednesday I would be doing a solo spin.

At first I thought I must have heard him wrong. What did the words mean? Solo spin? He enlightened me. It was a legal requirement. He said I had to climb to 3,000 feet over the airfield and do two, three-turn spins - one in each direction - while he watched from the safety of the ground.

I spent the next forty-eight hours in dry-mouthed terror, and came close to abandoning aviation for ever. I won't bore you with my miserable mental state other than to mention that I struggled with ideas for avoiding my appointment with death. I could invent a mag-drop, or perhaps disappear behind the hills to the north, and return 20 minutes later declaring that I had done the deed.

When the time came, and the altimeter had crept it's way up to 7,100 feet, I resigned myself to the hereafter. I cleared the area, applied carb-heat, throttled back and raised the nose. At 40 mph I hauled the stick fully back, tramped on the left rudder and closed my eyes. After a while I remembered that I should do three turns. I opened my eyes and tried to concentrate on counting while the "T" shaped runways rotated in the windscreen. To my amazement when I used right rudder followed by stick forward, the airfield steadied itself and I eased out of the dive – still alive.

Your first solo is nothing compared with the first solo spin – it is the greatest confidence-builder in the world. I was a Lindbergh, a Wiley Post and a Howard Hughes. I could do anything with an aeroplane.

Such bravado is frightening, and had I been flying a less gentle aeroplane I would soon have killed myself with that sort of attitude.

Fortunately, before I had time to provoke fate with my Cub-induced overconfidence I found myself employed by Placo and flying as a dogsbody to Piet van der Woude and Zingi Harrison. They quickly put me in my place and I was able to learn, from the right hand seat of a Comanche, how survivors fly.

As a final comment on the Cub, here is what Max Stanley, Northrop's test pilot, said: "The Piper Cub is the safest aeroplane in the world – it can just barely kill you".

Of course all this flying had to be paid for, and a chicken farmer's salary doesn't go far when flying costs 10c a minute (R6 per hour).

I had to sell my TR3 that I had driven down from Kenya, and replace it with a motorcycle - a Matchless 500cc single - which I loved.

Then the flying club told me to apply, through them, for a Government Subsidy administered by the DCA (Department of Civil Aviation). I naturally applied, along with 23 other students. And guess what - we were awarded 24 subsidies. I was over the moon with excitement, until the secretary told me that one student had been given two. And I had got none.

When I wanted to make a fuss about it, the secretary suggested that I think carefully. With a name like Kennard-Davis I was wasting my time, and it would be a mistake to make enemies at DCA when my flying career was only just starting. Wise words.

But I had run out of money to feed my addiction. So I went to a marble-pillared bank in Pretoria and told them I needed the money, and as soon as I had my license I would get a flying job and start paying them back. I don't know whether I was more naive than them, because I believed what I was saying, and so did they.

It didn't occur to either of us that a PPL is not a license to fly for money.

Bossie, Bombdoors & Syd

The previous chapter was mostly about the little Cub on which I trained. Now I want to tell you more about the curious people who influenced this wonderful part of my life.

I can't say whether Bossie was a good instructor or not. We always think our own instructor is godlike. Hell, he has over 200 hours. How could he not be the master of all things aeronautical? However Bossie didn't always meet expectations - things tended to go wrong on his watch.

For instance there was the day when his training technique, combined with the terminal stupidity of a pimple-pushing potential pupe, grounded the whole of the Pretoria Flying Club's fleet in one fell swoop.

This spotty enthusiast arrived clutching a sweat-stained voucher, cut from the Pretoria News, which promised him a discount on his first flight. Bossie, wasting no time with briefings and pre-flight formalities, strapped the acne-encrusted youth into the rear of the Cub while muttering instructions on the operation of the heel brakes, the throttle and the mag switch.

In no time Bossie was swinging the prop of ZS-BNR, one of the club's yellow J3 Cubs. Fate was not smiling on him that morning. She had handed him a pupil with the intellect of a mangel-wurzel. However, to be fair, he had never even sat in an aeroplane before.

Had Bossie been more perceptive he might have noticed, while explaining the intricacies of prop swinging, that his customer's eyes glazed over like those of a hibernating reptile.

Folks who have been involved with hand-starting aeroplanes will remember that one has to observe certain formalities. The guy doing the swinging calls out when he wants the mags switched off and the throttle open, for blowing out; or the throttle set, and the mags on, for starting.

This proved a bit much for our bewildered enthusiast. His manipulation of the switch and the throttle somehow got out of sync with Bossie's requirements. His instructions conformed to his normal mode of address. "Switch the fokking mags on"... "not now, dodo — when I fokking tell you"... "set the fokking throttle"... "don't ask why - just fokking do it" ... and so on.

We the onlookers, were unaware of this confusion until, without warning, the engine suddenly took and rapidly accelerated to full power.

Now, a more alert pupil might consider closing the throttle as one of the options available to him. He might also turn the mags off, or use the brakes, but this lad was reluctant to fiddle with things he didn't understand. He adopted the passive role of a spectator and waited to see how events would develop.

In fairness, we must remember that our hero had no way of knowing the difference between normal and abnormal activities as far as aeroplanes are concerned. So in his mind the interesting proceedings may have been pretty much what was expected.

Bossie, on the other hand, realised that the time for action was upon him. He sprang to the left to avoid being eaten by the prop. He then grabbed the strut in an effort to restrain the aircraft before it gathered too much speed and perhaps took the passive pupe on a premature first solo.

Unfortunately, this sort of incident was not uncommon in the days before aeroplanes were fitted with electric starters. From time to time one would see a man frantically tugging at the strut or wing-tip while the aircraft circled noisily around him.

Our pupil was either unable to hear, or couldn't understand Bossie's bellowed instructions, for he stared rigidly ahead and refused to get involved. We could see Bossie's energy beginning to flag. He knew this couldn't go on forever. It was time for desperate measures. He had no option but to attempt a do-or-die manoeuvre which he knew had little chance of success.

He abandoned the strut and dived for the cockpit. It was a hopeless gesture. The Cub got away from him, but instead of heading out across the field, it rapidly gained momentum in the direction of its home base - like a mongoose scuttling to the safety of its burrow. Its aim was unwavering as it sailed straight through the open doors of the Pretoria Flying Club hangar.

The scene of devastation inside was total. Most of the Club's fleet, consisting of another Cub, a Trike and a 140 Cherokee, were mangled to various degrees. Eventually the Cub's wooden prop broke and the engine thrashed itself to death. In the appalling silence that followed, the pupil was heard to ask, "Can I come next week then?"

***

Misfortune seemed to be part of Dirty Bossie's life. Some time later, when I was working as hangar-boy for Placo, he staggered into the crew-room looking, if possible, even less washed than usual. His shirt was torn and streaked with grass-stains, his bare arms were scraped and covered in red dust, and a trickle of blood ran from his matted hair down the side of his face.

"A good night out, Bossie?" someone asked.

After a bit of coaxing the story came out. Bossie and a pupil were taxiing a Tiger across the rough, brown grass when the tailwheel fell off. This wasn't as uncommon as one might have liked. The normal procedure on such occasions was to chuck the tailwheel in the boot, move the pupe to the front seat, and the instructor would lift the tail to shoulder height. The student would then apply just enough throttle to keep things moving. In this way one 'taxied' the aircraft down to the maintenance hangar.

Bossie, while conforming to this tradition, had a number of factors conspiring against him. One was that when one or both of the main wheels stop against a tuft of grass, massive amounts of power are needed to get the show on the road again. Another is that a Tiger is on the point of balance when its tail is lifted to shoulder height. A little higher and the weight of the top wings and the fuel tank moves ahead of the main wheels and she tends to nose over. The third, and in this case, most serious problem was that the person 'manipulating the controls,' (as the Air Law books would have it), would not be one's first choice of control manipulators.

Exactly how these factors combined to sabotage Bossie's efforts is not recorded. What is known is that there were many bursts of almost full power which hurled sand and dust into the face and clothing of the hapless Bossie. It seems that one such burst was combined with some forward stick - to keep the weight of the tail off Bossie's shoulder. Perhaps Bossie suffered a moment of inattention while he twisted his head in an attempt to wipe the gravel from his eye against his sleeve. Anyhow, a combination of all these factors was enough to do the trick.

The tail started rising, got past the point of balance, and rose even more strongly - with Bossie still attached. There was an explosive crashing as the wooden prop ripped into the ground and sprayed splinters across the airfield. Bossie hung on valiantly until the tail swept through the zenith of its arc, at which point he released his grip and was catapulted into the dirt some distance ahead of the now inverted Tiger and pupil.

He recovered consciousness within seconds, rose to his feet and staggered back to the crew-room nursing that aggrieved spaniel look.

Before leaving Dirty Bossie, I should point out that he was not to be confused with Dirty Potty. Many will remember Dirty Potty for his superb aerobatics in Tigers, Chippies and Harvards. He was said to be able to kick up spray from the wingtip of a Harvard while doing steep turns over Hartbeespoort dam. He was not unwashed, he was known as 'Dirty' because of his willingness to bed any female person, of any age, at any time and anywhere.

* * *

Then, in total contrast to the malodorous Bossie, we had the bristly little Major Bomb-Doors Pidsley, who was determined to get a bit of good old-fashioned discipline into us.

The Major had that stiff, military, no-nonsense, shoulders-back air about him. He cultivated a seven-aside ginger moustache. He always introduced himself as "Pidsley. That's - Papa India Delta Sierra Lima Echo Yankee" – a habit which caused us to question his sanity.

He was outraged that on the downwind leg we didn't really do any checks - mainly because there was nothing really to check.

This situation offended his military soul. His Air Force background caused him to view our lack of activity on downwind as a grievous affront to his professionalism. He therefore imported, from his war-time days, a list of things that might demand the attention of a Lancaster bomber pilot.

When we flew with him, we were obliged to recite these bomber checks which had nothing to do with a Cub.

Thus, all the way along the downwind leg we would bellow, at the back of his head, a litany of things that didn't need doing. The final item on this checklist was 'bomb-doors'. I am still not sure whether they were meant to be open or closed.

Not surprisingly the Major, who became known as 'Bomb-doors Pidsley', instilled in us a massive contempt for checklists. An attitude which came close to killing me a couple of years later. I will tell you about that when we get there.

* * *

Then there was the Amazing Sid Excell. He wasn't an instructor, but he was one of the folks who made up that colourful bunch of pilots at the time.

I first met Syd in 1963. I was driving to Wonderboom in my open, red MG TA when I spotted this tall, straggly, white-haired figure striding along the verge. I drove to alongside and opened the door. "G'morning, Sir, may I offer you a lift?"

"Fuck off," he said. "I'm exercising".

My next encounter with him was no more cheerful. Zingi and I entered the tearoom verandah and were greeted by Syd and invited to join him and the young lady who was with him. Once we were settled I politely asked if I could fetch a drink for Syd or his daughter.

"Fuck off." He said, this time without explanation. So I left the happy throng and went on my way. Obviously it was someone else's daughter.

Zingi clarified matters later, "Davis, you spastic oaf, that's his screw, not his daughter. Now sit down and let me tell you about Syd, and his nine lives." Nine wives, I thought was more like it.

Zingi then related a number of Syd's exploits. Some were so extraordinary as to be almost unbelievable. Others consisted of throw-away lines like, "He pranged a DC2 killing all on board, but Syd walked out without a scratch." Exactly how he accomplished this feat was not explained.

Then there was the time when he was flying a De Havelland DH89 Dragon Rapide - a 6-8 seat biplane twin, with Gypsy Queen engines. His mission was to transport a number of 4 gallon tins of ghee, a type of cooking fat, between two inhospitable points somewhere in North Africa.

The afternoon was hot, the turbulence uncomfortable and the tins of ghee were not tied down.

A desert whirly-gig caught Syd unawares and lifted the nose of the Rapide. Before he could react, the ghee migrated aft to the extent that he couldn't get the nose down.

The Rapide shuddered into a stall, dropped a wing and started spinning vigorously. Syd's best efforts to recover made no difference. He decided to unbuckle his seatbelt, go back into the cabin, and rearrange the cargo.

While he was thus occupied the Rapide sailed into the desert floor.

After the dust settled, there was little to be seen of the Rapide. There was a small pile of wreckage, and Syd sitting on a tin of ghee, waiting to be rescued.

Next he did a magnificent job of ditching a Dak into the Mediterranean on a pitch-black night. There was so little damage that the aircraft, with empty tanks, stayed on top of the calm water. At dawn, the crew were astounded to see the shoreline less than half a mile away.

Syd, being the captain, lead the way. He ran along the wing and executed a spectacular swallow-dive – into about 3 feet of water, almost breaking his neck. The rest of the crew waded to the beach while Syd recuperated in the Dak, and waited for a boat to transport him ashore in a more dignified manner.

After the war Syd was involved with the formation of Trek Airways, which had connections with Luxavia. This avoided apartheid sanctions. Trek eventually became Flitestar.

Syd used to corner me in the tearoom and mutter darkly about the dirty dealings of the government, the Broederbond, and people in high places. He was always on the verge of toppling the government by revealing its foul secrets. All this was given to me in a stage whisper with Syd nervously glancing over his shoulder.

In fact there was good reason to take Syd seriously – he was a loose cannon of note.

On one occasion, he set up a meeting with the Commissioner for Civil Aviation, Colonel Frank Elliott-Wilson. Syd was in dispute with the Colonel over the renewal of his (Syd's) Senior Commercial License. The meeting took an interesting turn when Colonel Elliott-Wilson confirmed that he was not going to renew Syd's licence.

This pissed off Syd to the extent that he pulled out a 45 revolver and let loose at the Commissioner. Not one or two, but the whole six shots were dispatched in the direction of the now moving target. Elliott-Wilson, although no youngster, put on a surprising turn of speed as he galloped round the room with bullets thudding into the furniture and walls.

Hardly had the fun started than the police burst in and put a stop to it. They slapped handcuffs onto the defiant Syd, and dragged him off to the lockup.

A swarthy contingent of cops had been lurking in the dark passage outside the Commissioner's office. The surprising thing was that the cops were there because Syd had suggested their attendance. He had tipped them off, that morning, telling them they would hear something of interest if they lurked and listened at Elliott-Wilson's door.

Syd soon found himself in the Pretoria Supreme Court charged with attempted murder. Valiantly refusing the court's offer of legal representation, he conducted his own defense.

Syd called his only witness, a Mr. du Plessis. And addressed him as follows.

"Are you Mr. Johan Jacobus du Plessis?"

"I am."

"What is your profession, Mr. du Plessis?"

"I am the manager of the Lynwood branch of the Standard Bank."

"Mr. du Plessis, do you have in your possession a sealed envelope that I gave to you for safe-keeping on the 22nd of September 1958, the day before my alleged attempted murder of Colonel Elliott-Wilson?"

"I do."

"Would you please read the letter to the court?"

"The letter says, 'I, Sydney Excell, intend to shoot *near* Mr.. Elliott-Wilson in order to frighten him.'"

After much commotion and protests from the prosecutor, the court was adjourned for an Inspection In Loco. This means you all troop off somewhere to view the evidence. In this case the venue was a shooting range, and the purpose of the visit was to see whether the accused, Captain Sydney Excell, had the ability to shoot near, rather than at, Commissioners. In other words they were there to witness Syd's prowess with a 45 revolver.

It turned out he was an excellent marksman, and the court conceded that he could indeed have plugged the Commissioner in the eyeball had he so desired.

Interestingly, after these events, Syd's license was swiftly renewed.

* * *

These stories are all true. I don't have the imagination to invent them.

* * *

PPL, Placo, Hired and Fired

I don't know whether training was different in those days, all I can say is that my own was very unlike modern PPL training. My logbook shows that I got my license at exactly 40 hours, which included a 30-minute flight-test and the six and-a-half hours I wasted in Nairobi with Mr. Tuckwell.

So my 'proper' training at the Pretoria Flying Club consisted of 13h 20m dual, and 20h 10m solo. There were no lectures, briefings, or debriefings of any kind. And the little bit of knowledge I acquired to pass the written exam was gleaned from Dave Worthington's 'Private Pilot's Handbook' and a couple of Birch and Bramson books - all borrowed.

Much of my solo time was acquired after Dirty Bossie had said, "What do you want to do today?" To which I would reply, "Stalls, steep turns and forced landings", or some such nonsense. This would give me cart blanche to disappear and do whatever I wanted.

I twice came close to killing myself on these jaunts. The first was when I went and circled my wife on the chicken farm. The house was on the side of a hill, which meant that in order to stay low enough to be really impressive, my circles were conducted partly uphill and partly going down.

Any pilot will tell you that going uphill and turning in a 65 hp Cub, at that altitude, is pretty suicidal. I had no knowledge of such things and was therefore somewhat exasperated by the little aeroplane's crappy behaviour.

It kept going all floppy and dropping a wing. Eventually I gave up and took it back to base to have it seen to. It was plainly suffering from some mechanical malady. Obviously none was found.

The second nonsense occurred, just after I had finished reading Paul Brickhill's brilliant book, 'The Dam Busters'.

Suddenly I am not Jim flying a Piper Cub, I am Guy Gibson, flying O for Orange, a Mark III Lancaster of 617 Squadron.

I swoop down to 60ft so that the twin spotlight beams combine to form a circle on the water. I aim for the middle of the Möhne Dam wall. Tracers from the towers stream directly at me and skim just past the cockpit. The aircraft rocks in the night sky as bursts of flack get dangerously close.

Actually that is not quite true. I have the Cub at 10ft above the waters of the Bronkhorstspruit Dam. At the last second I pull up and rocket over the wall at all of 70 mph. What a man.

I have 32hrs in my logbook and I am invincible. When I tell my buddy about it he wants to know whether I went under or over the wires that run from one tower to the other. "Wires?" I say, "What wires?"

Actually I didn't see much wrong with it, apart from the fact that I had no dual training on low flying. Oh yes, and you're not allowed to do it solo.

Then there was another big event in my training - my solo cross-country. Because there were no lectures or briefings, the word 'cloud' meant nothing to me. They were simply nice cotton wool things which I had never encountered at close quarters.

The terms VFR, instrument flying, graveyard spiral, and so on had never been part of my vocabulary, so I had no fear of clouds.

I did two unbelievably pansy dual cross-countries. The first was to Bronkhorstspruit, Rust de Winter Dam and back. Never more than about 40 nautical miles from base. The second was the same trip the other way round. 1h 10m and 1h 05m respectively.

After this Bossie considered me capable of flying to the little town of Brits, thence to Baragwanath airfield, and back to Wonderboom. All on my own.

Met reports were not part of his somewhat grass-roots approach to aviation. He simply told me that if I could see the Albert Hertzog tower I would be close to Baragwanath... "Now bugger off".

The information about the Hertzog tower was of course absolute hogwash. The ghastly edifice is nearly 800 ft tall and can be seen from almost anywhere in the greater Johannesburg area.

Actually despite the inaccuracy of Bossie's statement, it proved surprisingly useful. Here's what happened.

I could hardly fail to find Britz - it is only a few miles outside the Wonderboom circuit. All went splendidly until I was about half an hour out of Baragwanath, when a solid layer of low cloud appeared below me. I pressed on in blissful ignorance. I saw the top of the tower poking through the cloud, and when my watch said my ETA was nearly up, I simply descended into the cloud.

The sensation was a little odd as I peered over the side in the hopes of spotting a landmark through the soup. Then our motion started to feel distinctly peculiar, and the wind noise became shriller.

Just then a tiled rooftop appeared close to the left wing-tip, which was banked well down. I levelled off, waited for the compass to stop swinging and turned gently on to my previous heading. I was still not in the least concerned as I skimmed 20 ft above the rooftops.

Suddenly a Dak loomed out of the mist. Gee, I thought, the weather must be bad if a Dak lands on a road. I had better do the same. Which I did. The road turned out to be the main runway at Baragwanath.

When I taxied up to the fuel pump Mike van Ginkle appeared out of the mist, like the Dak, and asked me what the hell I thought I was doing flying in weather like this, where the hell I had come from. "Wonderboom" I replied innocently.

"Don't move," he said, and stormed off to phone my instructor. An hour or two later the weather cleared and I flew back to Wonderboom none the wiser. I had no idea that I had done anything stupid, let alone illegal. And life-threatening.

Bossie was a wonderful character – but not the greatest instructor in the world.

Looking back, what little learning happened on my way to a PPL, mostly happened when the Cub and I were aloft on our own, and the grimy but good-natured Bossie was drinking coffee in the clubhouse.

* * *

Suddenly I had a passport into aviation. It was a small, black, hard-covered book that proclaimed to the world that I was a Pilot.

Armed with this and my logbook, showing exactly 40 hours, I went to Placo (Pretoria Light Aircraft Company), the Piper distributor for southern Africa, and marched confidently up to the main office door.

I was greeted with a big smile by a guy in a white shirt and a bow tie. He told me that he was Zingi Harrison, the Sales Director, and asked if I wanted to buy an aeroplane.

When I told him that I was available for employment and held out my license and logbook as evidence, Zingi's manner changed abruptly. After a quick glance at my documents he curled his lip, adjusted his bow-tie, and told me to fuck off and get some flying experience.

My life fell apart. I had never doubted that once I had my PPL I would leave chickens and become part of the flying world. Besides, I had no money to pay for more flying; yet without the extra hours I would be farming chickens for ever.

I had to find someone with a solution to my problem. I phoned everyone I could think of. Eventually I spoke to a friend of a friend – a man named Hugh Stocks who had also dreamed of flying when he was young. He now owned a magnificent twin-engined Aero Commander 500B, ZS-CTC, which he flew to Kimberley once a week on business.

Hugh turned out to be one of life's gentlemen. He invited me to fly his young airliner, as it seemed to me, from the left-hand seat. He had an Instructor Rating, so I could log the hours.

One night we were on long final for runway 11 at Wonderboom, when the flare path and city lights started rotating around the aircraft. It was terrifying. I immediately asked Hugh to fly.

The problem was simple. I had a cold, and had decided to hold my nose and blow, to relieve the pressure in my ears. It was a massive lesson. I learned that flying with a cold can kill you - day or night.

The memory of Hugh Stocks and his kindness, has since nudged me into passing his humanity on to other youngsters needing a leg-up on to the bottom rung.

In a month I flew 15h 40m in Hugh's Aero Commander.

This, together with a sort of dumb perseverance, caused me to go to Placo once a week and hang around outside Zingi's office. Eventually it paid off. Zingi told me to report for duty on Monday. I was to be a hangar-boy-cum-trainee salesman.

Years later he told me he had only given me the job because anyone that persistent had to be a good salesman. He was wrong – I turned out to be an abysmal salesman.

My salary was to be 40 Rands a month - about half of what an apprentice bank clerk would earn.

It's my first day at Placo, take-off is set for sunrise. Our destination is Mafeking – over the western horizon. Old Piet, who is 'Ze Boss', has decreed, "Ve are leaving at six o'clock in ze morning, in Charlie Visky Golf". So I am there an hour beforehand to open the hangar doors, do a pre-flight, and wheel the 250 Comanche outside in preparation for his Highness.

It is the most beautiful machine I have ever seen. It is red and white and the inside smells of leather. It is hard to believe that I will soon be travelling in this miracle aircraft. I am much awed by the mass of dials, gauges, levers and switches.

My duties with the company include making tea, polishing the outsides of aircraft, hoovering the insides, and blacking their tyres. Zingi has told me that I will occasionally fly with the big boss. It seems he is scared of having a heart-attack or something, and likes to have another pilot with him. I know that my meagre skills will do little more than postpone our deaths should Old Piet collapse at the helm.

Anyhow, about two hours after our ETD, (Estimated Time of Departure), the great man arrives in his black and chrome Buick, in a cloud of red dust. He eases his bulk out of the car and views me with the sort of detached curiosity one might employ when sighting a distasteful exhibit at an art gallery.

He is of heavy build and medium height. His suit is clean and obviously expensive, yet he has the appearance of one who has spent the night inspecting a drainage system. The whole assembly is topped off with a sweat-stained brown hat.

Pieter van der Woude, known as Mr. Piet, is from Holland and has never lost the accent.

Mr. Piet   Zingi   Jim

He surveys me with a distant contempt. Finally he recognises me and his thoughts fall into place, "Hell's teeth, Zim, ve are late." He makes it sound like my fault.

We clamber aboard and are soon rumbling down the taxiway to zero-six. "Vot's our heading?" he enquires.

I am baffled by this question. I have only a remote idea where Mafeking is. Besides, I consider my status to be that of a passenger, yet he seems to want an answer with numbers in it. My idiot expression prompts further enquiry, "Vare's ze map?" I grope around the cockpit looking for some concealed map compartment. Meanwhile Mr. Piet does a 180 and we thunder back to the hanger. "Zere is a map on ze crew-room vall." I take the hint and dash inside while he and the Comanche growl on the tarmac.

There is a piece of string and a Douglas protractor nailed to the wall-map. I pull the string across to Mafeking, read off 270, and sprint back to present this figure to my fuming employer.

Soon we are in the air and heading west.

Now there is one thing that Mr. Piet does to perfection - getting the aircraft trimmed in level flight. The manifold pressure and revs quiver exactly on their assigned digits, the mixture is tweaked with a jeweller's precision, and the final trim adjustments are done with delicate taps of the middle finger on the overhead handle. The result is that the Comanche tucks its nose down and really gets moving.

Having set it up, he indicates that I should take the controls. He says nothing; he simply points at the altimeter and the directional gyro, and I know that it is my duty to maintain a heading of 270 degrees and flight-level 85. Old Piet then retires behind his newspaper and makes cigar smells.

I hold the required numbers as accurately as I can. I crave recognition - some word of approval that might indicate my job is secure. I want to do this forever. Old Piet seems to have lost interest in our progress through the atmosphere. I take this as a small gesture of his confidence in me.

Now, it is 180 miles from Wonderboom to Mafeking, and we cruise at 180 mph. From this, it is obvious, even to me, that our trip should take about an hour.

After 55 minutes Mr. Piet lowers his newspaper and peers over the top of his half-moon glasses. "Vare ze hell are ve?" he enquires. I am beginning to wonder about this myself. It is a spectacular day – you can see 60 miles to the horizon in any direction, yet the desolate countryside is devoid of any interesting feature - it is particularly devoid of Mafeking.

"Ve vill give it anozer ten minutes," he proclaims, as if warning the landscape itself. I know that should this delinquent town fail to appear within the allocated time, I will be held responsible.

This is indeed the case. Mr. Piet employs harsh words to describe my ancestors, my education and my intelligence. We are obliged to land in a field, to "Ask some bastard ze vay".

The bastard points North and we blast off again in that direction and soon reached our destination. Enroute, old Piet seems to be brooding on some weighty matter. There is an air of disharmony in the cockpit.

"Vot about ze bloody variation?" he asks.

I am intrigued by this seemingly new topic. Anything to take my mind off the shame of my navigational ineptitude. Variation is a noun that has a familiar ring, but its significance eludes my troubled brain. I am keen to learn more, and wait for him to continue on this subject.

"Zim, you are fired."

This lump of information is something of a conversation stopper. It keeps me quiet for the rest of the day.

We land back at headquarters that evening. Zingi comes out to greet us. Even at the end of a hot day he looks cool in his crisp white shirt and polka-dot bow-tie. "Zingi," Piet says, "yesterday you employed zis bastard, and today I fire him". He stomps off.

Zingi descends on me like the twin towers. Then he reminds me that 24° of westerly variation are not just words – they have meaning that apparently even bees cannot ignore when transitioning between their home and selected morsels of flora. He advises me to keep a low profile for a few days.

I think Zingi is the greatest guy on earth.

<u>Note for non-pilots</u>: Variation is a part of normal Navigation unless you live in England, where it is so small it is negligible. In South Africa it varies from approx. 22deg to 25 deg West. Maps are printed pointing to True North. Aeroplanes have Magnetic Compasses... Variation is the difference between the position of Magnetic North and True North. Since Magnetic North is West of True North in South Africa, and Pilots fly directions based on the Magnetic Compass, SA Pilots need to add the Variation to the True heading in order to reach their destination. This is part of the normal Navigation Training for PPLs.

Old Piet, Mr. Piper and Eric

The day after Old Piet fired me, and Zingi un-fired me, I am about to climb aboard my Matchless to go home, when Zingi shouts to me from his office, "See you at the Hunter's." I realise this is not an invitation but an order to meet him at the pub at the end of the road.

We settle on the verandah. Zingi's tall, amber glass drips condensation as he leans back comfortably. I sit on the front of my chair holding a Coke bottle in both hands and wondering what this is about. I am far too lowly a being to mingle with Zingi on a social level. "Relax," he says, "I'm going to tell you a story about Mr. Piet, so you understand how Placo works."

He is about to pull me into line. He gave me the job, so my miserable performance is a reflection on him.

Here is the story that Zingi told me on the verandah of the Hunter's Retreat in the fading light.

At the end of WWII Zingi and Piet were both young Second Lieutenants in the South African Air Force. One moment they were zipping through the Mediterranean skies in their Spitfires, and the next they were unemployed.

Zingi and Piet were saying goodbye on the smoky platform of the Pretoria railway station. Each had their worldly goods in a kit-bag, and £20 a piece in their pockets – a gratuity paid by the SAAF.

The train gently hissed steam as Zingi climbed aboard – he was going to the coast to look for a flying job. Piet said he was heading for America, where he planned to get the Piper aircraft agency for Southern Africa.

Piet took the train to Cape Town. Then he walked to the docks where he found an unpaid job as second-radio-operator on a ship bound for the USA. The trip took four long weeks before they docked in New York.

Next, Piet hitch-hiked 200 miles inland to the little town of Lock Haven, in Pennsylvania, the home of the Piper Aircraft Corporation.

Piet's timing couldn't have been better. William T Piper had been building Cubs flat out for the army and air force. Suddenly the war was over and he found himself with acres of aeroplanes and no customers. The military didn't need them, and civilians had no money. Piper was facing ruin.

When his secretary buzzed to say she had a South African in the waiting-room who wanted to buy 300 aeroplanes, Mr. Piper put the champagne on ice and gave his visitor a royal welcome. However, his joy soon evaporated when Piet explained that he possessed nothing more than £12 left over from his gratuity.

Piet said he would like to take the aircraft to South Africa and sell them. He promised to pay Mr. Piper for each one as he sold it.

Amazingly William T Piper and Pieter van der Woude shook hands on this outrageous proposal. It turned out to be the best deal each had ever made. For many years Piet's company, Placo (the Pretoria Light Aircraft Company), was the world's best-selling Piper dealership outside the USA. Old Piet and William T Piper were to remain firm friends for the next 25 years until Piper died in 1970.

Piet now had 300 aeroplanes in America, and no money to get them to South Africa. Also no one was lending money just after the war. But Piet could see no problem. He bought a ship, promising to pay the owner when he reached Cape Town. Then he hired a crew off the dockside in New York and promised to pay them when they reached Cape Town.

They loaded Piet's 300 Cubs and set sail across the Atlantic.

When they docked in Cape Town Piet sold the ship for enough money to pay the previous owner, pay off the crew, pay the railways for taking his aeroplanes to Pretoria, and rent a hangar. He then stripped 50 Cubs and put the parts in boxes – for spares. He sold the remaining 250 aircraft, one at a time, for £425 each. That was about half the price of a fancy motor car, so they sold extremely well.

Every time he sold an aeroplane Piet would send Mr. Piper his £420, and put the remaining £5 profit in his back pocket. But the real profits rolled in when his customers needed spares and maintenance.

Back on the veranda at the Hunter's, there is only a glow where the sun had been. Zingi downs the rest of his beer and wipes the back of his hand across his mouth. He suggests that I let the history of Placo seep into my soul. He urges me to use it as a guide for my future thoughts and actions.

As he goes down the wooden steps he pauses and half turns, "Whatever you do in life, give it a full go." I watch as he moves across the lawn and fades into the darkness.

* * *

I take Zingi's advice and work hard. In less than a year I have my Commercial Licence – suddenly I am the most highly qualified – and worst paid – pilot in the company, and I am still a useless salesman.

But I am getting ahead of myself. My time at Placo was the most stimulating and exciting part of my flying career. This was a boom-time for aviation, and the industry attracted wonderfully colourful characters. Some were ex WWII military pilots who wiped their bums with the restrictive civil aviation laws. There were rogues, villains and cowboys - everyone seemed to be larger than life.

Some attached themselves to aviation because there where easy pickings amongst the monied folk who bought aeroplanes. In fact Placo employed a salesman in this category. A man who will go down in history as being one of the world's best con men. He was also unbelievably charming and good looking. I guess people have to like you before they trust you with their money.

And so, with a fanfare, I introduce Eric Owen Winson.

Eric, sometimes known as Farley, was a well-built, dark, handsome brute of about 30. He could, and did, literally charm the pants off every pretty girl within a 100 miles of wherever he happened to be that particular evening.

He was by far the best salesman Placo ever employed, before or since. At that time we were selling about one new aircraft a month. When Old Piet and Zingi pushed off to the Piper factory for a conference, Eric said to Dronkie Lombard, the other salesman, and myself, "Right, guys, let's empty the hangar before they get back."

And that's exactly what we did - we sold ten aircraft that month. Two new ones, and eight were second-hand. We sold the whole damn lot before our amazed bosses returned. I say 'we' but that's a lie - it was all Eric's work. I couldn't sell a life-belt to a drowning man, and Dronkie lived up to his name - he was drunk for pretty much the entire month.

But despite Eric's amazing ability as a salesman, he much preferred conning people - it was an irresistible challenge, which he enjoyed far more fun than making an honest living.

The first big scam that I knew about was when there was a horrific drought in the Northern Transvaal. There were sickening pictures in the newspapers of cattle dying of starvation.

Eric searched out the phone numbers for all the main ranchers in the area. He called each with the same story. He was an animal lover, and he was appalled by the terrible pictures. He owned many acres of green pastures in Natal. If the farmers would care to rail the cattle down, he would feed them and send them back when the drought was over.

Of course they were delighted. There were no receipts or anything, because Eric was doing them a favour.

As the trainloads of cattle arrived in Pretoria, Eric diverted them off to the abattoir and pocketed the loot. Naturally when the rains came and the farmers wanted their cattle back, Eric simply said "What cattle?"

However, most of his dealings were not agricultural, although he did sell Old Piet's Comanche ZS-CWG to the fertiliser baron - and later rugby boss - Louis Luyt. I remember hiding nearby in the shadows in the hangar, to watch Eric's sales technique.

He seated Louis in the red-leather interior of the Comanche, while he painted a fairy-tale picture for his customer. Louis would be flying to Lourenço Marques for an illicit, romantic weekend. He would have his golf clubs in the back of the aircraft and his gorgeous partner in the right hand seat as they slid serenely over small patches of cloud. They could just see the pristine white beaches and the palm trees in the distance.

Louis couldn't sign quick enough.

Eric didn't sell aeroplanes - he sold dreams. And he did it extraordinarily well.

He would sometimes disappear to the Free State for a week and come back with an Aztec sale which was always subject to a couple of conditions such as marrying the buyer's daughter and somehow gyppoing the HP company so that Eric's own wallet bulged rather than anyone else's.

The farmer, his wife, the HP company, and the farmer's daughter were always the losers.

He was careful to involve the farmer in some form of slightly illegal activity. He might inflate the price of the aircraft and use the extra to up the farmer's deposit. Or there might be some tax dodging. That way, when the farmer eventually realised that things were going off the rails, he could hardly run to the cops and admit his complicity in the various frauds.

But even the best of schemes must come to an end. You can't do this sort of thing too often before the law starts to catch up on you, and eventually Eric headed for South America two steps ahead of a stream of creditors. And taking with him a spectacular blonde whose sister happened to be married to Zingi's brother, Barry.

The next we heard was that he had been jailed in Argentina for pushing his baby, in a pram, across the border. Not a serious crime, you might say, and one would have to agree with you - except the baby happened to be lying on several million dollars' worth of counterfeit money.

I am not making this up - it is in the court records. In Eric's application for a firearm license, in the USA, he omitted to mention he had been jailed. Inevitably, they caught up with him.

Eric escaped from jail, we never heard exactly how. Then Barry, I think it was, spotted an extremely luxurious yacht at Monte Carlo, and commented that it must belong to Aristotle Onassis. "No," came the reply, "It belongs to a bloke called Eric Winson."

* * *

But I must tell you of about an incident when Eric saved my life.

It was late afternoon. I had just returned from a few days at Westminster, in the Free State, trying to sell a Tri-Pacer to a farmer. That is a story in itself, mainly because I actually succeeded - not through any ability on my part, but due to the incredible strength of that ugly little aeroplane. I'll tell you about it later.

When I landed at headquarters that evening I discovered the hangar looking like a Christmas tree.

There were strings of coloured lights everywhere. Around the walls there were tables decked with white linen, champagne glasses and mountains of food. At the back there was a well-stocked bar.

And, in the centre of the hangar, lit up by spotlights, stood the sleekest and most magnificent aeroplane in the world. It was the first Twin Comanche in Africa, and it had been flown in a few days earlier by the great Max Conrad, setter of many world endurance and distance records.

It was to be a flag-waving event for Placo and Piper Aircraft. The Mayor of Pretoria was the guest of honour. Important people would make speeches and it would be in all the newspapers. It would also make headlines in South Africa's only flying magazine *Wings over Africa*, whose editor, John Chilwell, owned a Tri-Pacer, and was a big Piper fan.

Anyhow, I was on the apron, admiring the presentation when Mr. Piet, the big boss, walked over.

"Get zose bastards out of my hangar," he said.

At first, the words meant nothing to me. I thought he was talking to some unseen bystander lurking in the shadows. When the penny dropped, I realised he was referring to three unshaven guys in leather jackets, who were standing around the bar, having a quiet drink and enjoying the snacks.

I was mystified. "Do you mean I should ask them to leave?"

"Zat bloody murderer is not bringing his gangsters to drink my fucking hooch."

"Murderer?"

"Johnny Vilkinson."

"He's a murderer?"

"Sure he is. Now get ze bastards out."

In those days murder was still considered a fairly serious offence in South Africa. Wilkinson had kicked one of his mates to death while attending a jolly motorcycle jamboree. I naturally felt a certain reluctance to break up his little get-together.

While gathering my thoughts I remembered that Eric, who had been a Rhodesian middle-weight boxing champion, lived on the airfield.

I legged it round to his residence and battered frantically on the door. "Eric, Johnny Wilkinson and a couple of his buddies are drinking Mr. Piet's champers and he wants you to get them out of his hangar." I lied.

"No sweat," said Eric, dabbing on the last few drops of aftershave, and straightening his tie.

We headed for the hanger, in the fading light, me lagging a couple of steps behind. As we got there Eric said, "Leave this to me."

I assured him I would try to hold myself back from getting involved in the forthcoming interview. In fact it would be a huge pleasure. I watched from the shadows as he strode into the hangar and straight up to the murderer and his cohorts.

Eric spoke earnestly to him for a few minutes, and then the three thugs departed the scene. I was astounded. "What the hell did you say to them?" I asked.

"I told Johnnie we were expecting some rough elements to gate-crash the celebrations, and I employed him as our chucker-outer."

The first thing he did was boot his two mates out, and then disappear. He returned a short while later, all shaved and spruced up, wearing a penguin suit, which Eric had loaned him.

He behaved immaculately all evening and no doubt concluded a couple of mutually profitable deals with Eric.

What a wonderfully loveable character that Eric was. He died in the USA in 2009 at the age of 77.

Flying with Mr. Piet

After Old Piet had got over his initial spate of firing me, I found myself with the dubious honour of being his constant co-pilot, and bag carrier.

Although this seemed like a fairly permanent arrangement, an air of disharmony always permeated our shared cockpit. I soon learned that he marched to the beat of his own drum. I simply followed, trying to keep in step. This was not easy because I seldom heard the drum - he never told me what was going on. It simply didn't occur to him that our agenda could be any of my business. Naturally this led to some difficult moments.

For instance, on our first trip to Lourenço Marques (now Maputo), as we were descending towards the coast in his 250 Comanche ZS-CWG, he broke a long silence. "Vare is your Passporto?"

"Passporto?" I enquired. I had reason to be perplexed because he hadn't told me we were going to foreign lands. His mood was not improved because I have an annoying habit of looking like a stunned ox on such occasions.

"Your Pass-bloody-porto." He repeated loudly.

"Ah. Well now - that would be at home, then."

This brought on one of his tirades. They invariably started with "Hell's teeth, Zim, you useless bastard..." He would then go on to mention such topics as my education, my failure to grasp even the simplest of concepts, and in particular, my ineptitude for anything to do with aviation. It often ended with an appeal to the heavens. "Ye Gods, vhy do you punish me viz zis spastic?"

I eventually became hardened to this form of abuse, so long as it didn't include the word *fired*.

Anyhow, once we had agreed that I had no passport or visa to enter Mozambique, he then instructed me that, when interrogated by the 'Passporto Gestapo', I was to employ my stunned ox expression, and say nothing. He would handle matters from thereon.

On the ground, a moustachioed man with an important hat predicted that I would spend much of my future in a Portuguese jail.

I did the ox thing, and Piet said he would enjoy a quiet chat with the moustache in a back room. They soon emerged, all smiles. The Gestapo stamped a visa into my pilot licence, and we went on our way.

We did many subsequent trips to Mozambique, where we sold a surprisingly large number of aircraft. I soon learned that all types of officials, or Gestapo, as he called them, invariably smiled when they saw Mr. Piet.

Our return to Wonderboom from such trips was always interesting, and sometimes bloody dangerous.

The problem was that most aircraft didn't have radios. So we would often return to find the circuit alive with Cubs, Tigers and Aroncas, doing their beautifully square training circuits. If Schalk Barnard, the Air Traffic Controller, happened to be on duty, in his wooden box on bricks, he would use his Aldis lamp to give signals to the aircraft that didn't have radios – which was most of them. Otherwise they were just left to sort themselves selves out with Mk 1 eyeballs,(old Military term for keeping a bloody good lookout).

Piet's circuit-joining procedure was somewhat unusual. When we were about five minutes out he would switch on the Narco Omnigator, and allow time for the valves to warm up. He would then dial in 118.1, Wonderboom's frequency, pull out the whistle-stop, which was used to match the received signal to the transmitted one. There was a coffee-grinder handle on the right-hand side and you wound this until the thing made a piercing shriek - which confirmed that it was ready to go. All you had to do was get rid of the noise by pushing in the whistle-stop, and go ahead with your message.

Piet regarded Wonderboom as his own private airfield. He had actually started it some years previously. The fact that it now belonged to the Municipality did nothing to alter Piet's impression that all other traffic was there at his pleasure, or displeasure.

He would then announce our presence by saying, "Vonderboom, Vonderboom, zis is Charlie Visky Golf. Ve are coming in on 24."

He gave no information about where we were coming from, or what sort of plan we had for getting on to finals for 24.

The broadcast was delivered in the manner of a benevolent dictator, and was issued as a friendly warning to the controller to get his house in order in preparation for our arrival. Unfortunately the call was always made at such short notice that the wretched Schalk could only stare in horror as we sailed through his circuit, often against the prevailing traffic. Even if he had time to reply, it would have been useless because Piet invariably switched the radio off as soon as he had delivered his bomb-shell.

Then he would turn to me and say, "Zim, votch out for cowboys. Zese bastards are going to cause an accident pretty soon."

His choice of runway was seldom dictated by the wind, or the position of the sun - it was generally the one straight ahead, depending on where we had come from.

Piet's landings were unbelievably bad. They were said to have caused so many back-injuries that the local chiropractors paid him a commission. Still, they were never responsible for any actual bloodshed, and our aeroplanes stayed in one piece - so I suppose we were flying strong aircraft.

His landing technique was to throw the whole lot at the ground with such force and determination that a bounce was out of the question.

We came back from Lourenço Marques one afternoon. Piet had spent most of the previous night at the fábrica da cerveja

– the MacMahon beer factory – getting himself outside a substantial quantity of their excellent product, and several plates of prawns. He now had the air of one whose central nervous system had been subjected to a Fukushima-like event.

I was generally only permitted to fly straight-and-level, but on this occasion he inclined his throbbing head to indicate that I should reduce the noise-level and commence the descent. I was further led to believe that it was my privilege to join the circuit and establish us on finals.

Even then he made no move to take command of the proceedings. It seemed that, unbelievably, he was going to give me a landing. "I'll show the old bastard how to land an aircraft", I thought. It went perfectly. I had everything rounded-out and floating a few inches above the centreline. The nose was coming up smoothly for a greaser on the main-wheels. Suddenly there was an explosion in my left ear and the stick was slammed hard forward. "Vot ze hell do you sink you are doing?" he bellowed as the aircraft smashed into the ground in true Piet style. "Are you trying to kill us all?"

As we taxied in he seemed pleased with the results of his quick thinking. "You must votch out for zat sort of sing," he explained.

Piet claimed to hold the record for short landings - 78 yards in an Aztec! When questioned about the circumstances he became evasive on the quality of the landing - but insisted that the distance was accurate.

I later learned that on this occasion, he had failed to deploy the undercarriage.

* * *

A Bug in the Cockpit

I am sure that he didn't wake up in the morning and say "I have just thought of a new way of killing Davis", but it certainly seemed like that sometimes.

Old Piet and I had a very peculiar relationship. He was God, the boss and founder of the company. He was a massive extrovert who could achieve anything and turn the world inside out. I held the lowest and most humble position both in Placo and in the aviation industry. I was Piet's, and everyone else's, dogsbody, and willingly did whatever was necessary to hang on to my tenuous position at the bottom of the ladder.

When I say tenuous that's what I mean. Piet fired me on my first day at work, and both he and Zingi fired me on several other occasions.

When Piet employed me his reason for having me fly with him was that he was scared of collapsing with some physical ailment. He wanted another pilot to either die with him, or land him safely and summons medical assistance. Since the little bit of flying I had was mostly in Cubs equipped with 5 instruments, and since I was now flying in Piet's Comanche that had a cockpit similar to that of the older generation Boeings, any expectation that I might get us safely on the ground was pure whistling in the dark.

Piet plainly did not enjoy my company, so I quickly learned not to chirp. This made life difficult because he seldom spoke to me, other than to berate me for failing to anticipate his requirements. Such was my fear of the great man that I seldom even asked where we might be going or whether we would be returning within the forcseeable future.

Navigation was largely a matter of pointing the aircraft in roughly the right direction and then making occasional reference to a BP, (PB Petrol Station), road map, which I was never allowed to examine. This meant that I spent much of my time speculating about both my short- and long-term future.

This lack of comms led to a number of embarrassments. Apart from the one mentioned earlier, there was the time when I was arrested by that branch of the civil service which he referred to as the polícia Gestapo. Piet, his son-in-law Jon and I were in the open-air bar of the Penguin Club in the red-light district of Lourenço Marques.

Piet and Jon were at a table near the exit and I was at the bar. A lady-of-the-night was being a little over-persistent in the promotion of her merchandise. After several unsuccessful attempts to persuade her to take her trade elsewhere, I lost patience and dumped the entire contents of my almost-full beer tankard over her head.

This turned out to be a bad move.

I am a bit of a slow thinker, so I had difficulty in organizing my thoughts around the events that followed immediately upon my dousing act. There was screaming, the clattering of booted feet on the cobbles, the rear view of Old Piet and Jon legging it down an alley, and the piercing screech of police whistles.

I was bundled off my bar-stool by two smelly, unshaven, uniformed people who were particularly muscular around the neck and shoulder areas. As I was being dragged up the road, Piet and Jon appeared from their alley. Piet immediately entered negotiations with the Gestapo. Some escudos changed hands and I was released into the custody of my employer, who was instructed to keep me under control.

As time passed and I gained flying experience Piet's opinion of my aeronautical skills seemed to diminish to new depths with each additional hour that I logged. He almost never trusted me with a take-off or a landing, and preferred to use the autopilot in between, so I felt about as useful as a second navel.

Actually, as I saw more of his flying I often wondered about his ability to get us safely on the ground, even on the rare occasions when he was feeling fine and had no hangover.

By normal standards I would not say Piet was a good pilot. His checks and procedures were worse than appalling – they simply didn't exist, and his handling of the aircraft, particularly his landings, would make brave men weep. All his flying, including the final approach, was done with his feet flat on the floor. They would only be lifted on to the rudders at the moment of touch down.

He saw himself as invincible. He had supreme confidence in his ability to achieve whatever he wanted, so he gave no more attention to flying an aeroplane than he did to squashing a bug.

In fact, bugs were fairly high on his list of things that did get Piet's attention.

He suffered from entomophobia, meaning he had a thing about goggas, a disorder that was to bring us both to the brink of death.

To defend himself against creepy-crawlies, Piet always carried a brown-paper bag containing DDT, a banned, white, toxic powder. If he considered himself to be endangered by an ant or mealy-bug, for instance, Piet would simply unfurl the top of his bag and sprinkle some of its contents on the offending invertebrate.

There is, however, a time and place for everything. Joining the circuit at Lourenço Marques is neither the time nor the place to be powder sprinkling, so it's unfortunate that a member of the arthropod clan should choose this moment to announce its presence by becoming airborne in the cockpit.

Such was old Piet's enthusiasm for slaughtering these pests that it absorbed his entire concentration. He was like a bloodhound. Once he was on the chase nothing else mattered. The fact that we were descending at 200 miles per hour into a busy circuit was wiped clean off the slate of old

Piet's consciousness. He was suddenly not a pilot, but a pest exterminator on a mission.

"You vork ze levers, and I'll kill ze bastard" he said, handing over control of the Comanche.

By the time he opened his bag of DDT and had it at the ready, the unsuspecting insect was peacefully sunning itself and preening its whiskers on the glare-shield above the instrument panel.

It is hard to know exactly how the first dollop of powder affected the creature. One can only speculate that its interest in feeler cleaning was replaced by a sensation of resentment or displeasure. It quite understandably developed a desire to be elsewhere. Searching for a more peaceful location on our planet, it took off and initiated a recce of the windscreen area hoping to find a path to greener pastures. Piet, in his enthusiasm for the hunt, was now applying the entomological equivalent of the saturation bombing that the Allies employed against Hitler during WW2.

The inside of the Comanche soon resembled an explosion in a flour factory. In fact, such an event would have been a huge pleasure compared with the handfuls of deadly talcum that Piet was hurling round the cockpit like a drunk in charge of the confetti basket at a wedding.

Initially he didn't seem to notice that we humans were taking more of a battering from crossfire than the solitary member of the enemy contingent.

Within seconds we were so overcome by the stifling dust that I, at least, lost all interest in the offending creature. Indeed, our paroxysms of eye-watering, coughing, sneezing and choking left no room for other activities. Even, our progress through the busy circuit was of no interest compared with our need for lungfuls of clean air. However, Piet retained his single-minded determination to slaughter the intruder.

When I was finally able to devote some attention to the circuit, and the other traffic, the situation had worsened. Some trick of science had caused our passage through the tropical air to generate a form of static electricity that attracts molecules of powder to Perspex. The result was an opaque layer, like frost, that clung to the inside of all the windows. This effectively put us in IMC.

ATC interrupted our misery to inform us that they would enjoy a chat with us in the tower, if we were able to regain control of the aircraft and conduct a safe return to the planet.

I was obliged to fly on instruments while Piet improved visibility and ventilation by opening the storm-window and using his sweaty hat to rub peep-holes in the windscreen.

This was one of the few landings that I was allowed to do uninterrupted. The old guy was preoccupied with poking around under our seats and on the floor. As I brought the aircraft to a halt in front of the marshaller, Piet surfaced and announced, triumphantly dangling the now deceased organism by one feeler in front of me, "Got ze bastard!"

Komatipoort to Stegi

It is really not nice to say that someone was a terrible pilot. And perhaps it was not even true of Old Piet, because he died in his bed. He flew, or rather drove, the aeroplane without feeling, or finesse, and his checks and procedures simply didn't exist.

This story, which my logbook tells me happened in a brief 30-minute flight, is an indication of his competence in the cockpit. The date was the 1st of November 1963, and we were flying Piet's new Twin Comanche ZS-DPI.

We had landed at Komatipoort to clear customs, for a short flight to Stegi (now Siteki) in Swaziland. When we came to take off, Old Piet just rammed the throttles forward and clenched the stick with both hands. He was much given to this get-in-and-go attitude. I had still to learn that pre-take-off formalities in the cockpit were to be my department - in the interests of self-preservation. At that stage however, I was far too lowly a pilot to interfere in the operation of twin-engine aeroplanes.

Due to the fact that we were still trailing full flap, a legacy from the landing, our acceleration was somewhat below par. Even in those days Komati had miles of dirt runway, so I kept my peace on the assumption that we must eventually fly. I was, in fact, partially correct. By the time we hit 85 the tail was flying, the main wheels were off the ground, and the nose wheel was grinding itself into the dirt.

Piet decided this was the right time to get the rest of the aircraft flying, so he issued his usual command, "Come to Papa," as he hauled on the pole. The main wheels slammed into the ground, but apart from that not much seemed to happen.

By now we had used up a lot of runway, so I ventured my solution to the problem. "Mr. Piet, we still have full flaps."

He hit the flaps off and we sailed into the air. Instead of thanking me for my alertness and presence of mind, he let loose with, "Hell´s teeth, Zim. Vot do you sink I employ you for - your good looks?"

He then went on to describe, in some detail, how I was expected to justify my slender pay-packet. It seemed that my duties were many and varied. He mentioned that he was not greatly interested in the quality of the tea that I made for Zingi. And that the blackness of the polish I put on the aeroplanes' tyres did not excite him. The cleanliness of the hangar floor was only of passing interest compared to my number-one-duty - that of keeping-the-boss-alive-by-remembering-what-he-forgets.

Because it is only a short flight from Komatipoort to Stegi, there is no need to gain much height before levelling off. Old Piet kept up his tirade of scurrility throughout the careful process of adjusting the power, leaning the mixtures, and trimming. It was his pride to get every ounce of cruise performance out of an aircraft. When he had finished, we were settled down nicely at about 40 mph less than our normal cruise speed. The reason was perfectly clear - he had been so busy berating me that he had forgotten to pull up the undercarriage.

Now, compared with some of Piet's blunders, this was a minor error, of little consequence. However, although not dangerous in itself, it is the sort of thing that makes the perpetrator feel somewhat foolish.

I was obliged to point out that Piet's omission was the reason for our dismal progress through the sky. This sent him off on another onslaught on the subject of my parentage and various other previously omitted factors which he felt contributed to my generally defective character. "Hell's teeth Zim, you stupid bastard, vot have I just been telling you…?" He carried on for a while and eventually lapsed into a sulky silence.

A familiar air of disharmony permeated the cockpit. I fumed inwardly and resolved to teach the old bugger a lesson at the first opportunity. As it happened my chance to educate him arrived within minutes.

The geography of our destination was such that it was necessary to beat up Mr.s Viggie's hotel, before landing on the golf course. The good lady's name was actually Mr.s Wigman, and the hotel is still there, some half a century later. It is situated in the bottom of a hole that had been cut out of a forest of tall gum-trees. The idea was that, on hearing us, Mr.s Viggie would fire up her aged Ford truck and collect us on the fourteenth green.

As the old guy eased the nose down towards the trees, I knew it was time to put into practice all the advice he had just given me. "Mr. Piet we must change tanks now." I ventured this proposal for the very good reason that the gauges showed zero on the tanks we were using.

"Who ze hell is flying zis bloody sing?" he asked.

So we stayed on the empty tanks, with predictable results.

Now when a fuel-injected engine starts to die of thirst, it doesn't just peacefully expire, it has several false stops interspersed by bursts of power. As the engine gives up, the aircraft swings violently towards it. This is counteracted by a bootful of opposite rudder, which often coincides with its recovery, causing an even more violent swing in the other direction.

When both engines quit simultaneously, the bursts of power, swinging and kicking of rudder present an unusual spectacle to the casual observer on the ground. But to the more involved spectators aboard, it causes a frightening demonstration of chaos in the cockpit.

We go through the swinging and kicking procedure with hands and feet all over the place. Piet yells useless pieces of advice like "Hell's teeth Zim, vot ze bloody hell have you done now?... I'll change ze tanks while you hit ze pumps... For Christ´s sake keep ze bloody sing straight..."

We restore sanity to the machine a few feet above the trees. A perspiring Piet pushes his hat to the back of his head, beams at me and says, "Zat vos interesting, Zim."

One might think that things could not get much worse on that particular flight. But one would be wrong.

The word arrival is often used to portray a really bad landing. It is hopelessly inadequate to describe Piet's collision with the golf course. In fact there were a number of impact points, in a zigzag pattern, down the length of the fairway. Golfers and caddies scattered like chickens in the path of a Harley Davidson. Each time we struck the surface and sailed into the air Piet bellowed like a stricken water-buffalo. "Bloody hell... now vot?... look out Zim." We eventually ran out of steam near the blue-gums at the far end.

Old Piet hauled the mixtures back and let the engines shudder to a stop. In the comparative silence as they ticked out their heat, and we could hear the gyros starting to wind down, Piet turned to face me, and with a huge smile asked, "Vosn't zat a greaser?"

I could cheerfully have strangled him.

The morning after a night at Mr.s Viggie's hotel was always a dangerous time.

The dedicated student of survival will drink as little as is polite, go to bed early, wake up early, and take a brisk walk through the cold morning air to the golf course. This will sharpen one´s wits for the task ahead. You then do a careful preflight and some unorthodox cockpit preparation.

When Ze Boss arrives, it is a simple matter for him to strap himself in, hit the starters, cast a bleary eye round the cockpit and declare that "All ze clocks seem to be vorking. Ve go." He would then firewall the throttles.

* * *

The Pay Rise

Old Piet is a funny sort of guy. For one thing he is terrified of commercial airlines, so when he has to go off to the States for a Piper convention or something, Zingi asks if he will be flying there.

"Not a damn," he says, "Zose bloody sings can kill you. I'm going by B.O.A.T." For newer generations, B.O.A.C. (British Overseas Airways Corporation) was the previous name of British Airways.

Anyhow, while he is away, Myrtle breezes into the hangar. She is Piet's wife. She has sleek black hair in a Jackie Kennedy style and is stunningly beautiful. "How much is my husband paying you?" she asks.

"Forty Rand a month." I tell her. At the time this was about half of what an acne infested first-year postal clerk was earning.

"But you have a wife and child to support."

I admit the truth of this, but explain that my salary more than matches my worth to the company. I sense that she is not happy with this situation - she has the air of one who is about to poke a stick into a hornets´ nest, so I beg her to leave well alone. I explain that I have already been fired once and fear that the mere mention of my name may bring on another sacking attack.

"I'll speak to Mr. Piet about this," she says, and glistens out.

A few days later I am in the hangar applying black shoe polish to the tyres of a new Comanche when I hear the clatter of Zingi opening the window which connects his office to the hangar. Previous experience tells me that when I hear Zingi´s window clatter, trouble is not far away.

"Davis," he bellows, "what the hell have you done now?" I am much puzzled by the question, I can think of nothing I have done recently that might cause him distress. However it is not always easy to know with Zingi. A few days earlier I had been subjected to a demeaning bout of verbal abuse simply for answering his phone while he was out of the office.

A voice had said that I should give Zingi the following message, "Fred´s uncle phoned." Now, I had previous experience of giving Zingi incomplete messages and failing to get phone numbers, and it had not been pleasant. So I pressed the caller for more information. But all he would say was, "For Christ´s sake just tell him that Fred´s uncle phoned."

I was in a cleft stick: any more backchat from me and the dreaded uncle would blow a gasket and tell Zingi that I was an incompetent oaf, which he already knew. On the other hand if I failed to get a number I could expect a period of wretchedness to follow.

I tried a more oblique approach and enquired whether Zingi would know who Fred was. There was a gasp of despair and the phone went dead.

Not wishing to entrust such an important message to memory, I took out a new sheet of paper and wrote the following on it. "Zingi, Fred´s uncle phoned. Jim."

That afternoon I heard the clatter of Zingi opening his window, followed by the familiar bellow, "Davis". I dropped my tin of polish and zigzagged through the aeroplanes with all due speed.

"What the hell is this?" he enquired, brandishing my note through the window. It seemed fairly clear to me what it was, however I was reluctant to point out this obvious fact. So I put on my bovine expression and simply stared stupidly at him.

He tried a different approach, "Who the hell´s Fred?"

Ah, now this was easy - I explained that Fred was the nephew of the guy who had phoned.

Zingi was giving an impression of a dinner guest who had got a chicken bone stuck in his throat. His face was turning red and he was tugging at his bow tie in order to loosen up the airway. "Why didn't you get his number?" His voice had gone all quiet, like that of a Sergeant Major who is preparing for the big blast. I was starting to feel extremely uncomfortable. In desperation, I resorted to what I believed was a simple explanation of the whole matter.

"He told me you would know who Fred's uncle was."

"Davis, you microbe. That must have been Fred Zunkle."

"That´s what I said, Skipper."

"Get the hell out of my sight."

"Sure, Skipper." I said. I was becoming increasingly worried about Zingi's mental health.

All this is a bit of background to show that the sound of Zingi´s window opening and his enquiry into one's recent activities can cause even the most innocent hangar-boy a certain amount of apprehension.

"What the hell have you done now?"

I tell him that I don't recall any recent misdemeanours.

"Well something's up. Mr. Piet wants to see you."

I hurry across to the boss's outer office to be greeted by Molly van Blerk and her massive wobbling bodice. She was later to be flung in the slammer for stealing Piet's money. Anyhow she tells me to go straight in.

I knock and go quietly into his office. Mr. Piet does not give the impression of someone who wants to see me. In fact he looks like a boss who would be very happy if he never saw me again.

"Myrtle tells me zat I must pay you more money or fire you again." He rubs his chin and stares at me with watery blue eyes over his half-moon glasses. I feel like some vile insect that he has spotted crawling out from under his lettuce. He is obviously waiting for me to offer an explanation for this outrage. As so often happens, the situation seems out of my hands, so I just gaze miserably at the carpet.

"Vell," he says, "I sink I vill pay you an extra five Rands every monse." He makes it sound as if he is giving me a Lear Jet.

I leave his office knowing that I would gladly lay down my life for such a man. Actually he had already made several attempts to shorten my life, and I had no reason to expect a change in the near future.

Hypoxia

Clouds and turbulence were two things that really terrified old Piet. His efforts to avoid these hazards were sometimes so drastic they precipitated situations even more lethal than those we were trying to avoid.

Because of this perfectly justified fear of weather, one would think he would be keen to find out from Met what was expected – and then avoid it. I was once stupid enough to ask him if he had phoned for a Met report.

"And vot bloody good is zat going to do?"

I mumbled something about being better informed on what to expect.

"And you sink you can believe zose bastards?"

That pretty much put the lid on us ever discussing our future with the Met office.

In retrospect, the whole thing was highly hazardous, partly because he had no idea of what weather lay ahead, and partly because he was inconsistent in his methods of dealing with whatever the gods hurled at us.

On one occasion we were trying to get back to Wonderboom from Mozambique. Piet decided we would take our chances underneath a nasty looking lump of weather. He took scud-running to a new level when we were forced lower and lower by the cloud base.

Finally, I remember being in the bottom of a valley with the cloud just above us, and massive drops of rain splattering against the windscreen so we could see almost nothing ahead. Part of the problem was that Piet had said, "Ve had better slow zis bloody sing down in case ve bump into somesing." So we brought the twin back to about 90 knots with full flap. This meant that, with no prop ahead of us to blow the windscreen clean, we could only watch the rocky valley walls going past the side windows.

I was too inexperienced to be frightened, but Piet must have realised the seriousness of our situation. "OK Zim, you must help me now."

He told me to put my hands and feet on the controls. I don't know how this was meant to help. Then he commanded, "You votch zose clocks, and I'll votch zese vuns." This meant he kept an eye on the flying instruments, while I surveyed the engine gauges. Again, I have no idea why.

Oh, and just to make sure, he engaged the autopilot. This meant that all his inputs were simply fighting the autopilot. Eventually we found Marble Hall and bunked down for the night.

Soon after this, my logbook tells me that on the 11th of April 1964, we were cruising down the coast, from Vilanculos to Lourenço Marques. Our steed was a Twin Comanche, N7339Y. This was totally illegal because neither of us had American licences. A few fair-weather Cu's started to form ahead of us.

Now, this would have been the day for staying underneath it and following the beach, but no, our previous flight in the valley had so affected my boss that he decided to climb over the clouds. Naturally there were more ahead, and they were larger and thicker, so we kept climbing.

Soon the cloud was solid and continuing to develop vertically. To hasten our ascent into the thin air we wound in the Rajay turbochargers. As we sailed through 15,000 ft I remembered that one's finger nails should turn blue - as a warning that the respiratory system was taking a hammering. This was indeed the case - we both had blue nails and maroon lips. At 18,000 ft I ventured to point out this colourful phenomenon.

"Who ze hell cares about zat ven ze whole vorld is full of colour?" he asked. We were flying a pink aircraft through a yellow sky. We giggled and marvelled at the splendour of it all. At 19,000 ft we were behaving like revellers returning from a rugby match.

Eventually a crack developed in our new found friendship. I decided that, with an outside temperature of minus 20°C, it was time to do battle with the Janitrol heater. This is a malevolent device which lurks in the nose of the aircraft. It draws fuel from the right main tank and causes a young Guy Fawkes scene which is meant to transmit warmth and comfort to those in the cabin. Smoke it often causes; warmth sometimes. But there are few pilots who could claim to be comfortable with a petrol fire in the nose. Piet is not one of them. Knowing his distrust of the machine, I contrived to distract his attention while attempting to ignite it.

Perhaps it is fortunate that he saw through my ploy. These heaters, although sometimes effective in skilled hands, can fill the cockpit with more smoke than heat if the light-up procedure is attempted by an inept operator – me, for example.

"Vot ze bloody hell are you doing viz zat sing?" he enquired. "Are you trying to kill us again?"

Leaning over to my side to switch off the offending heater, he neatly inverted us into the cloud tops.

I have to admit that I don't remember how we eventually emerged safely – but emerge we did. And having got it shiny side up and pretty much under control, Piet initiated a now familiar monologue which touched on my education, the Neanderthals, from whom I was descended, the size of my brain - which he compared unfavourably with that of a cockroach, and my future prospects at Placo should I ever again touch anything without first consulting him.

* * *

On Fire

Actually, N7339Y was this very same aeroplane that had been ferried from the USA only a few weeks earlier by the famous long-distance record-setter, Max Conrad.

It was the first Twin Comanche in the country and, as the Piper distributors for southern Africa, we were naturally excited about its arrival. We were clustered around Wonderboom's box-on-bricks control tower. Zingi, bow-tie spruced up, paced around puffing on a stream of Lexingtons, and kept demanding that the brow-beaten ATC, Schalk Barnard, try to contact the aircraft every couple of minutes.

Eventually, as we stared at the evening sky to the north-west, we all spotted it pretty much simultaneously. But there was something very wrong – the aircraft was streaming a smudge of black smoke behind it.

Zingi, quick as a flash, dived into the tower, grabbed the mike and shouted, "November 7339 Yankee, you are on fire!"

After a moment's silence we hear a very bored accent drawling, "I yam naat on fiya."

Zingi: "39 Yankee, I say again you are on fire. You are trailing black smoke."

Max Conrad, now sounding seriously pissed off, said, "And I say again, I yam NAAAAT on fiya."

The poor man, then well into his 70s, had flown all the way down Africa with everyone telling him he was on fire. Of course the trouble had been the misbehaving Janitrol heater. The very one that I was playing with at 19,000 feet.

Actually, I had another nonsense with Zingi and a fire.

We had landed a 235, ZS-DUE, on the golf course in front of the Leisure Isle Hotel at Knysna. When I say "We..." I mean Zingi landed. He didn't trust me to do anything more exciting than hold straight and level, while cruising.

We stayed the night at Pat McClure's excellent establishment. Zingi was on top form in the pub, entertaining the locals – as only Zingi could – with story after story mostly about how he had done something stupid in an aeroplane. He had the stage presence to carry it off, to the extent that his status was enhanced rather than diminished by each new story.

The stories got better as the night wore on, and Zingi's delivery was improved with each Castle he put away.

Naturally, when it was time to head for East London in the morning, Zingi was little more than a cardboard cut-out of the man we had known the night before. He insisted that his headache was only tolerable if we brought the revs back to 1800. He also claimed it would improve with the intake of oxygen, so 500 feet was our ceiling for the flight.

As soon as he had the 235 set up he handed me the controls and told me not to wake him until I had East London in sight, or some desperate event took place.

As it turned out, both of these occurrences happened simultaneously. I spotted a large aircraft climbing out from East London, trailing an unbelievable mass of black smoke.

I was appalled. "Skipper, wake up – there's an aircraft on fire."

He was awake in an instant, like a snoozing cat that has had a glass of cold water chucked over it. Zingi grabbed the mike and shouted, "East London, Delta Uniform Echo, you have an aircraft on fire."

There was a slight pause and East London came back with, "No sir, that is one of the new Boeing Jet aircraft."

Zingi dropped the mike and stared at me, his eyebrows twitching, "Davis, you bastard..."

* * *

Hendrik and the Tiger

In order to explain Hendrik's fate, it is necessary that I first introduce Dronkie Lombard.

Dronkie had been bunged out of the South African Air Force because of his devotion to the bottle. You had to be pretty dedicated for this to happen – drinking was a compulsory part of service life, so to be heaved out for over-compliance meant that you were very serious indeed about alcohol.

Dronkie had a round, sombre face, and freckles to go with his ginger moustache and centre-parted ginger hair. He dressed immaculately, always wore a tie, and always smelled of mint. He seldom smiled and had a habit of glancing nervously over his shoulder as if expecting to be accosted by bandits.

I later discovered that it was, in fact, the police who kept Dronkie in a continual state of nervous tension, but that's another story, which I will tell you later.

Perhaps desperadoes were also after him because, after a few days' unexplained absence from work, he turned up at the airfield with a split lip, the remains of a black-eye, and his jaws wired together. Fortunately the undisclosed reason for his condition also caused the dislodgement of two front teeth. I say fortunately because this permitted him to drink soup through a straw. It also enabled him to maintain his intake of alcohol.

I don't wish to steal the limelight, but soon after Dronkie's tooth incident, I saved his life.

Turning up at an Air Force bash at Swartkop one night, I was making my way through the gardens towards the lights and music, when I heard a sort of gurgling whistle coming from the bushes. I quickly located the source of this extraordinary noise – it was Dronkie. He was hanging on to a branch of a thorn-tree while trying to empty the contents of his stomach onto the grass, through the gap in his teeth. Every so often the outlet became blocked by a lump of carrot or something, and this put him on the brink of drowning.

Realising that he needed a means of unclogging the orifice I plucked a thorn from the tree and handed it to him, thus saving his life, a service for which he never thanked me. But on with the story.

As the most junior member of staff, I was always delegated to do the crappiest flights. So, when a nine-hundred-mile trip across the desert to Windhoek, in a Tiger Moth, came up, I knew it was mine. I was therefore amazed to find Dronkie circling the Tiger in the back of the hangar, and casting a suspicious eye over it.

The grapevine soon confirmed that, as punishment for some alcohol-related indiscretion, he was to do the Windhoek trip. It was also revealed that he would be taking Hendrik, the other hangar-boy, with him to help with prop-swinging and refuelling en-route.

Hendrik was a smiling black man of average stature. His most remarkable feature was a pair of gleaming size 14 boots that gave him the appearance of one of those toys that swing upright if you push them over. We all liked Hendrik for his gentle disposition. Unfortunately he was a little slow off the mark – a characteristic which led to his downfall. Literally.

The great day arrived. Hendrik was wearing his blue work-overalls from the bottom of which protruded his glistening toe-caps. Dronkie was attired in a charcoal suit and paisley tie. They donned their leather helmets, climbed aboard the tatty yellow Tiger, and were soon a wobbly speck heading for the western horizon.

A few days later Dronkie returned on the DC4 milk-run. But there was no sign of Hendrik. Here's what happened.

Apparently all went well on the first day, but in the afternoon of the second, they picked up a ferocious wind which derailed their navigation, and caused them to divert to Mariental, for fuel.

It was blowing 40 knots slap across the sand runway. With no other options, Dronkie elected to land diagonally in the parking-area, in front of an open-shed hangar. This is not as stupid as it sounds because the aircraft would have a groundspeed of about five knots at touch-down.

On his first approach Dronkie managed to get the Tiger on the ground, but quickly realised that, with no one to hang on to a wing, it would be impossible to taxi to the hangar. He opened the throttle and was instantly airborne again.

During a turbulent circuit Dronkie explained to Hendrik, through the Gosport tube, that he, Hendrik, was to undo his seat belts, open the door and climb out on to the wing, while maintaining a firm grip on the centre-section struts. When the wheels touched, Hendrik was to leap off the back of the wing and grab the inter-plane strut, to prevent the aircraft from being blown over.

Hendrik didn't hesitate in this call to duty. As they turned final he was there, size 14s on the cat-walk and hands locked round the centre-section strut.

As they touched down two things went wrong simultaneously. Hendrik's built-in time-lag kicked in, causing an appreciable delay between Dronkie yelling "Jump" and Hendrik complying. The second problem was that the Tiger bounced. The result was that, by the time Hendrik stepped off the back of the wing, the Tiger was at about 15 feet.

A quick glance told Dronkie that his assistant would need a few moments to uncrumple himself before he could be relied upon for genuine assistance. So Dronkie did another circuit, landed close to the hangar where the hobbling Hendrik was able to grab the wing.

One would like to report that all's well that ends well, however that was not exactly the case.

The next morning, it seems that no amount of eloquence on Dronkie's part could persuade Hendrik to get back into the Tiger. Hendrik explained that his enthusiasm for aeronautics had diminished overnight. He stated that he has lost his ambition to be in the aviation business. An absence from anything to do with aeroplanes, he announced, would be an extremely pleasant state. He also declared that Mariental had a certain charm. It suited his disposition. He intended to retire there forthwith, and live out the rest of his days peacefully on the side of town most distant from the airstrip.

So now, when the occasional pilot who strays into Mariental for fuel asks about Hendrik, they are greeted with a blank stare. But should they mention his gleaming, footwear, then a smile of recognition will creep over the dusty features of the old refuelling guy.

* * *

Zingi and the Auster

I shouldn't moan about the R40 a month that old Piet paid me because part of the deal was that I also got a house, well a sort of house, on the airfield. Actually it was the paint-store belonging to Eddie Pelcher, from Republic Air Parts, before becoming my home. It was about 50 yards down from Placo's hangar.

Anyhow, that's where I lived with my wife and 3 year-old son. This is relevant to this story, so here we go.

Tea-making was one of the assignments at which I was particularly sharp. I could produce a cup of hot sustenance, to Zingi's formula, in less than a minute. I was busy with this duty when the window between his office and the hangar clattered open.

This was a chilling sound as it always seemed to precede a difference of opinion between myself and my short-tempered boss.

"Davis," Zingi yelled, "tell those bastards not to aim their aircraft at my hangar."

The mind raced. Our hangar must be the target of some sort of attack. I wasn't certain how I would repel the bastards, or deter them from their evil intent, but I was more than willing to answer the call to arms.

I dashed outside to assess the danger and to get a better view of the enemy, so as to formulate a plan that would put an end to their villainous aiming.

Looking where Zingi had pointed, I could see nothing more offensive than a couple of guys in the middle distance trying to start an Auster.

Thank God we are safe, I thought, and went back to report to Zingi that I could detect no evidence of any danger in our immediate future

Had Zingi not been Managing Director of Placo Sales, he could have taken up employment with any branch of the military that was in need of a Sergeant Major. His diction, volume and word choice would have fulfilled the most stringent demands of the job.

After adjusting his bow tie, he treated me to a sample of this talent, touching, as he often had before, on my genealogy, education, and resemblance to some vile creature in a pond. He also intimated that if I did not immediately get the Auster pointing in some other direction, he would perform bowl-surgery on me with a Comanche tow-bar.

This gave me considerable incentive, but it was still with a certain foreboding that I approached the perspiring pair of prop-swingers. They must have been at it for some time as the blazing sun was taking its toll on the bonhomie that is usual amongst pilots.

They viewed my approach without enthusiasm. My cheerful greeting and apologetic relaying of the boss's message did nothing to revive the joie de vivre that I expected.

Using an expression with sexual connotations, they invited me to go away.

Now I was in trouble – their suggestion was unambiguous, and yet Zingi had been more than clear about his requirements.

I shuffled hesitantly in no-man's-land, edging towards the hangar, hoping that Zingi had been called away on urgent business. He hadn't. He emerged from the shadows and stood, legs apart, gently swinging the aforementioned tow-bar. Even at that distance he seemed to have the disposition of a young Charlie-bravo. I could tell that if I wished to avoid the painful installation he proposed, I would do well to re-negotiate the matter with the Auster-swingers.

Tottering back to the front lines, I explained to the unhappy duo what Zingi proposed doing with the implement in his hand.

"Aha!" they said in unison, as if adding their approval and support of Zingi's plan.

The long and the short of it was that they finally agreed to let me help them turn the aircraft 30 degrees to the left – which meant that it was not technically aimed at the hangar

I returned to HQ with an air of rightful indignation. I had been subjected to considerable mental anguish while conducting a worthless project.

No sooner had I revived my tea-making activities when I heard the Auster start. After some introductory coughing and throat-clearing it settled down to a healthy roar. For God's sake throttle back, I muttered into the teapot. They didn't. The noise got louder and closer. There was a horrendous clatter and crash, a tinkling of broken glass, and then silence.

I stuck my head out of the hangar and was greeted by the sight of an Auster with its nose through my bedroom window.

Zingi followed me down to examine the damage. As he got there I looked round. Neither of us said a word, but the trace of a smile spread across his face as he lifted the tow-bar and gently waved it in my direction.

Now there was a guy who REALLY knew about aeroplanes.

(I am happy to report that no wives or children were harmed during the intrusion of the Auster into our home.)

* * *

Dendron

My logbook tells me that this next story had repercussions some 15 years later. So if you don't mind I will start at the end and then tell you what led up to it.

As I may have mentioned, I am proud to be a founder-member of the Live Cowards' Club.

There are only two rules: don't fly if something seems dodgy; and if you are flying, and something seems dodgy, land - gently.

So my story starts with me wandering around the airfield at Plettenburg Bay, waiting for my next student to arrive. Suddenly, from out of a crystal blue sky, a mate of mine, Carel van Aswegen, arrived in his little homebuilt, single-seater, *Bergwind*.

This threw me into a mild panic. I knew, with the certainty of déjà vu, that I would be forced to break rule 1. I could picture what was going to happen. Carel would spring out of his little aeroplane, stride across the grass, clap me on the back and say, "Take her up, Jim".

Carel sprang out of his little aeroplane, strode across the grass ...

To understand my predicament I must take you back to the beginning again when I was working for the greatest pilot in the world – Zingi Harrison

Zingi had flown spitfires in the war. Zingi could fly a Super Cub out of the hangar doors, and Zingi knew all there was to know about aviation.

This being so, I almost wet myself with excitement when Zingi told me I was to accompany him to an air show at the little farming town of Dendron. I could think of no greater thrill than to inspect, in his company,, such modern marvels as the Navion Rangemaster, the wooden-spared Mooney Master, and the S35, 'butterfly-tail' Bonanza.

All went well until noon when a thunderstorm hit the airfield at the exact time allocated to Dirty Potty's Amazing Low-Level Aerobatics Display.

Dirty Potty was the world's second-greatest pilot, after Zingi. The 'Dirty' part was nothing to do with being unwashed. It came from Potty's nocturnal activities. Not to put too fine a point on it, Potty was happy to bed anyone, anytime, anywhere.

But on with his aerobatics display. Potty somehow contrived to emerge from the bottom of the thunderstorm, amidst pelting rain and flashes of lightening. His Tiger was going downhill at an impossible angle, and the engine was howling as he disappeared behind a hangar.

I was in a state of horrified disbelief. On the one hand, I knew that the Great Dirty Potty was immortal – he couldn't crash a serviceable aeroplane. On the other hand my eyes told me that he must thud into the ground within seconds.

I couldn't believe it when, a couple of heartbeats later, the Tiger appeared from behind the hangar, now heading uphill at an increasingly steep angle, until it was inverted. Dirty Potty then pulled through to complete the loop, which again finished below the level of the hangar.

This was the start of the wildest low-level aerobatics display I have ever seen. Dirty Potty hurled the Tiger through a sequence of suicidal manoeuvres at such low level that the crowd alternately surged into the hangars for fear of being struck by the aircraft, then rushing into the downpour so as not to miss the next lightening-studded event.

As a finale, after once again herding us all indoors, Potty clattered the wheels of the Tiger along the corrugated-iron roof of the main hangar, kicking up such a racket that we all fled into the deluge again.

The storm and the aerobatics stopped simultaneously.

Next, a homebuilt aircraft arrived overhead. It was pitching up and down in a most alarming manner. As it joined downwind, Zingi dashed to the commentator's podium. He ripped the mike from the astonished broadcaster's hand and called for a doctor and an ambulance. I was as stunned as everyone else. Had Zingi lost it?

We soon found out. The oscillating aircraft smashed into the ground and disintegrated. A doctor attended to the stricken aviator, and the ambulance carted him off. We never heard whether he had lived through the event. The state of the aeroplane would indicate that he probably hadn't survived.

Zingi was carried shoulder-high and lauded as a hero. Here was a man who really knew about aeroplanes – he could even predict crashes.

One of the many pieces of wisdom that Zingi passed on to me was, "Never fly someone else's homebuilt".

Back to Carel and his homebuilt at Plettenburg Bay on the 6th of March 1978. I could find no excuse not to, so I reluctantly clambered aboard, with Zingi's spectre waving a finger of rebuke in my face.

Suddenly everything was OK – I couldn't get my long legs under the panel. "What a bastard," I said, "I'd just love to fly it, but I can't fit in."

"No sweat," said Carel, "lean forward and I'll take out the backrest".

This moved me back about 4 inches. Now I had no excuse.

As the wheels left the dirt I knew Zingi was right – I was going to die. I couldn't control the nose attitude. It went steeply up. I eased forward, and then more forward. But nothing happened. Then suddenly it pitched down – way too far. I quickly eased back, but again nothing, for most of the stick's travel, then bang, it was far too high again.

Throughout that terrifying circuit, I could see every detail of the Dendron crash. Carel's wretched Bergwind was behaving in exactly the same way. As it turned out I was just luckier with my landing, I managed to touch down at the bottom of one of its oscillations – no bloodshed or damage.

That was when I found something new to be cowardly about – it's this stupid phobia I have about flying with the C of G out of limits. Those 4 inches had been enough to turn a pussy-cat into a raging tiger.

* * *

The Moth and the Milk-Stool

Air Traffic Control at Wonderboom in the early 1960s was rather a hit-and-miss affair. There was a controller but he was an ordinary sort of guy with a requirement for ordinary bodily functions, so he wasn't always in his little wooden box on bricks. And even when he was there, he wasn't necessarily all there, if you follow me.

At one stage his job depressed him so much that he apparently ate a handful of pills and disappeared across the airfield to die. Zingi took off on the taxiway in a Super Cub and soon found the hapless ATC in the foetal position in the long grass. The doctor, who had been summonsed, took one look at him, and realised that no pills had been consumed, but rather that he suffered from a stomach ailment. He rather unkindly pushed a rubber pipe up the patient's bottom, and pumped some soapy water into him. It is the sort of activity that causes one to avoid doctors in the future.

Anyhow, the tower wasn't always occupied, and even when it was, most of us didn't have radios. If we were lucky we sometimes got a light from the tower – but mostly we just kept our eyes open and our mouths shut.

Anyway, Dronkie Lombard and I were leaning on the fence outside the crew-room. We watched idly as a blue Tri-Pacer, sometimes referred to as a Flying Milk Stool, entered our field of vision and taxied out.

Zingi joined us, lit a cigarette, straightened his bow tie and said, "This is going to be interesting".

I looked at him enquiringly. I was intrigued to know what he expected to be so engaging. "Why? What's going on, Skipper?"

"Davis – you useless bastard, don't chirp – just watch and learn."

As we watched, a curious series of events started to unfold. A Tiger Moth had lined up at the threshold of zero-six, and a glider was being attached to its rear. There was the usual assembly of towrope-checkers, canopy-closers, arm-wavers and wing-holders, each contributing their particular skills to the operation.

In the meantime the Tri-Pacer had taxied to the intersection and was about to backtrack when it noticed the Tiger at the threshold. The Tri-Pacer courteously elected to hold short of the runway to await further developments.

What we didn't know was that this was the Tri-Pacer pilot's very first flight after getting his PPL. He was taking his pretty, blond girlfriend along as his very first passenger.

Not wanting to waste time, the Tri-Pacer decided to do its pre-takeoff vital-actions at the intersection. We observed the stream of red dust that poured out behind as the mags were checked at 1800 revs. With these formalities complete, and still no apparent sign of action from the Tiger, the Tri-Pacer decided not to backtrack, but to set sail from its present position.

Now, the God who looks after drunks and pupil pilots, had recently been relieved of this responsibility because the student had become fully fledged PPL. He was no longer under the protective custody of the Almighty. With extreme bad fortune he managed to line up on the runway at the exact instant that the pilot of the Tiger, having received OK's from his assistants, opened the throttle to get the show on the road. Its own stream of red dust almost obscuring the glider.

We, as observers, at first found no cause for speculation. It seemed obvious that, although the Tiger pilot was blind ahead, with the tail-wheel rattling along the ground, and the nose pointing skywards, there was plenty of time for the Tri-Pacer to take off and leave a clear passage for the lumbering Tiger. Acceleration was slow in the hot 6000 ft density altitude.

Surely the Tri-Pacer would start moving at any moment. But we hadn't reckoned on the new pilot's conscientious attention to detail. Whatever other faults he may have had, he was not the sort of guy to be rushed. He was the kind of pilot who likes to have things exactly right. Having lined up he decided it was a good idea to go through his checks again. One would like to report that this pilot's thoroughness was a tribute to aviation safety - one would be wrong.

The duplicate checks take valuable time, and the Tiger has transitioned from a fast trot to a lolloping canter. The glider is airborne and the Tiger's tail is up. This affords its pilot an interesting view of the scenery ahead, and a particularly good view of the rear of the stationary Tri-Pacer, which grows steadily in his windscreen.

The term "on the horns of a dilemma" accurately described the Tiger pilot's predicament. If he closed the throttle, having no brakes, his momentum would probably still carry him into the Milk Stool. Besides, what would become of the flying glider in his mirror? But if he didn't abort the takeoff, and the Tri-Pacer continued its sedentary condition, the result was obvious.

As it turned out, the latter occurred. And so we witnessed the destruction of both aircraft.

The glider pilot jettisoned the towrope, flew over the scene of desolation and landed gently in the second half of the runway. Happily no one was physically hurt, although one hesitates to speculate upon the relationship between the Tri-Pacer pilot and the blonde.

It was hot in the sun so we wandered back inside. It's tough being a pilot when there is no flying going on. Besides it was nearly tea-time.

* * *

Too Stupid to be Scared

You know when you speak to an insurance company about comprehensive for your child's first car, and they go all thin-lipped and start putting Rand signs in front of telephone numbers? Well there are good reasons for that. Kids are stupid. They have no imagination. They are too dumb to be scared. And the male ones have testosterone coming out of their ears. Nothing going in.

And it's not only kids. Even at 24 I had no idea when to be frightened in an aeroplane.

Zingi had decreed that I should spend a couple of days serving a sort of salesman's apprenticeship to Erick Winson, the greatest salesman, and con-artist, in the world. We were to do a flag-waving trip round Natal and the Free State.

It was my job to watch Erick carefully, and absorb his technique. There was indeed much to watch and absorb. Erick always wore an immaculate safari suit, very shiny shoes, and aviator sunglasses. His black hair was slicked in place, and he had an arrow-straight parting on the left.

His handshake was firm and he looked you straight in the eye. When you spoke he listened as if you were the most important person in the world. And when he spoke it was always in calm, confident tones that told you you were in safe hands.

Had Eon Productions been auditioning for a James Bond they would have kicked the rest into touch when they spotted Erick.

Beside him, I was a bumbling idiot, an embarrassment, and certainly an impediment to his sales pitch. I'm sure he would rather I was elsewhere but he took my enforced presence graciously.

Our tour, in an almost new Tri-Pacer, took us over much of the Free State. Every now and then Erick would point over the side and say, "You see that place? That's Frikkie Odendaal's Farm. I sold him a 180 Cherokee last month, and bedded his daughter."

It appeared Erick had done a hell of a lot of selling and nesting in the Free State, and the same pattern extended into Natal. We night-stopped at Mtubatuba where Erick seemed to be something of a celebrity. I later learned that he was much admired wherever we landed.

He disappeared to stay with the rich and beautiful, while I dossed down at the Railway Hotel.

I don't remember much about the visit except that Erick came this close to killing us both.

An entourage of admirers came out to the airfield to see Erick off, and view the magnificent Tri-Pacer. Of course he had to take some of his potential customers for a flip. I was amazed how Mtuba was the home of so many latent aircraft buyers. Most of them seemed to be beautiful young women.

Eventually I was uploaded for our return to headquarters. After takeoff we built up a bit of height and then Erick decided his worshipers should be treated to a fly-past. He courteously asked if I was OK with this. "Of course," I mumbled, having no idea what he intended. I was, therefore totally unprepared for Erick's botched attempt at a wingover/stall-turn.

At the time I had 56 hours in my logbook and Erick had over 200 - making him a sky-god. Hell, he had more than enough to be a commercial pilot, so how could he get anything wrong?

Well he did.

We dived into the flypast at 150 mph (the red line is at 140). We pulled up almost vertically and then steeply over to the right and down towards the gum trees. I realised things might not be going exactly as planned when we sailed through the tops of the trees while being pushed into our seats by serious G. The manoeuvre bottomed out over the runway at shoulder height.

When I asked Erick if it was OK to fly through trees he said of course it was - but perhaps I shouldn't mention it to Zingi. He also pointed out that there was a 50% safety margin built into all aeroplane figures, so I shouldn't be worried about the airspeed.

I am a slow learner. It took me a long time to realise how close we had come to death that morning. As has happened to so many pilots, before and since, he simply overcooked a manoeuvre he didn't understand.

For me it was all a tremendous treat. In fact he let me fly all the way back while he slept off the previous night's excesses. And Erick didn't drink – but he was much into excesses.

The last part of our journey was in the dark. It didn't go too well initially because the gyro instruments had all mysteriously failed. They came back on line when Erick opened the storm window, leaned forward are removed lumps of vegetation from the venturi.

We flew just to the east of Jan Smuts, as it was then. We tried to raise them on the Narco VHF, coffee-grinder, but it was unserviceable. With those radios, that was their default condition.

Then we wound out the fishing reel in the roof in order to trail the HF aerial. We only had two HF frequencies – 5680 and 6552. And Smuts, didn't pick us up on either although we could actually see the flarepath and the tower. Eventually Salisbury, now Harare, replied and relayed our messages to Smuts. And so I learned about the capricious nature of HF radios!

Erick even gave me the night landing at Wonderboom, although I had no night rating or training in night flying. I suspect he was also not rated. Besides I think he was still considering our close call at Mtuba, and was wondering how he would explain to Zingi about bits of gumtree that were still attached to the aircraft.

After landing, Erick got Hendrick, the other hangar-boy, out of bed, and the pair of them spent some hours that night removing all trace of our agricultural incursion.

* * *

I then did about another 20 hours of Tri-Pacer flying. After this Bomb-doors Pidsley, (who used to introduce himself as Papa India Delta Sierra Lima Echo Yankee – confirming our belief that he was cookoo) insisted that I needed one-and-a-half hours of dual to convert me to a Colt, which is a two-seater Tri-Pacer without flaps. This sharpened my downwind checks considerably - I had completely forgotten the whole Lancaster bomber routine.

Next came a one-hour conversion with Mike Kemp, onto a 175 Cessna, ZS-CMR.. In fact it was the first Cessna I had ever flown. Neither of us had much enthusiasm for the brute with it's notoriously unreliable, high-revving engine, and geared prop. Not a nice aeroplane.

The purpose of this conversion was so that I could fly one back from Zeerust the next day. Erick had arranged some dark, private deal for a second-hand Mercedes to be delivered to a motor-dealer in that town, in exchange for some unnamed benefit to both parties. It was my privilege to drive this splendid vehicle there, and return with the 175.

I particularly remember this trip because I was again due to arrive back at Wonderboom after dark – still without a night rating.

It slowly dawned on me that I had a problem when I was about to make VHF contact with Wonderboom, I realised that I had no idea of the aircraft's registration. I hunted in all the pockets and the glove compartment, looking for some document that might reveal our identity. Nothing.

Now, a more seasoned pilot might simply have invented a registration and called Wonderboom using that pseudonym. It never occurred to me to lie on the radio, so my call went something like this:

"Wonderboom, this is er, um, thingy, I don't know my registration, on 118.1."

"Aircraft calling Wonderboom, say again your registration."

"I don't know my registration."

"Oh, for crying out loud, this is all I need at the end of a long day. What's your aircraft type?"

"A Cessna 175."

"OK, Cessna 175, go ahead."

* * *

Then a few days later, Bill Fortuin converted me onto a Super Cub, ZS-DRS, in preparation for a mammoth trip to Windhoek. More of that later.

But before the Windhoek trip, in fact on 15 December 1963, I flew with Zingi to Lobatsi, in the British protectorate of Bechuanaland, in a 235 Cherokee. This little town, which housed the BMC (Bechuanaland Meat Commission) and not much else, was very interesting for two reasons.

First, it was the base of operations for a huge androgynous German, named Herbert 'Bertie' Bartuane, who had previously flown for the Luftwaffe. When I met him he was flying a Ryan Navion with a 205HP Continental, which only just managed to grope its way off the ground on a hot day. In fact, Bertie's own massive pear-shaped structure made the carriage of fuel, passengers and luggage an extremely dodgy business.

The "Encyclopaedia of African Airlines" by Ben R Guttery, refers to Bertie and his business on page 26:

BECHUANALAND SAFARIS (1960)

Bechuanaland Safaris was founded by "Bertie" Bertuane as a charter company. His interests were acquired by the National Airways Corporation of South Africa, which operated the company as a subsidiary providing air taxi services and a small domestic network linking Francistown and Lobatse to Gaborone, Maun and Ghanzi, using a Piper PA-23 Aztec, and a Piper PA-23 Apache. [I came close to death in both of these aeroplanes at different times - I will tell you about them later.] *The carrier ceased operating at the end of 1965.*

As the Beechcraft distributors for Southern Africa, it must have stuck in their throat operating a couple of Pipers in and out of bush strips that the Barons simply couldn't handle.

I can't remember whether this visit to Lobatse was to persuade Bertie that he needed an Apache/Aztec, or whether we were demonstrating the 235 Cherokee to the other very interesting character there. I won't mention his name for fear of being shredded by his lawyers. And I will just call him Wilhelm.

The interesting thing about Wilhelm was that as soon as he got his brand-new 235, he stripped out all the passenger seats and much of the upholstery. It transpired that this was so that he could cram the aircraft full of lion skins - which he illegally flew into South Africa.

It wasn't long before the SA Police caught up with him. They dragged him off to court and fined him. But it seems he didn't get the message, because a few months later he was again caught, subjected to some demeaning finger-wagging and criticism from the bench, and slapped with an eye-watering fine.

Some people never learn, because the third time they nailed Wilhelm, the Judge barely took up the court's time. He simply confiscated the 235, emptied Wilhelm's piggy-bank and hurled him in chookie for six months.

When Wilhelm got out after only 3 months, because he behaved nicely, he gave up flying. You see, he didn't need to do it any more, he retired to his Sandton mansion and sipped champers next to the pool. His flying had been all about diamonds. The lion skins were just a cover.

* * *

Those were interesting days. While I am still thinking of it I must tell you about my near-death experience in Bertie's 235 Apache.

Zingi said, "Davis, get in the back of that aeroplane - we need some weight, and even you can't stuff up being heavy." Zingi had a way of making one feel useful.

Actually, I must sidestep for a moment to tell you a quick story about that.

Zingi stuck his head into the crew-room, "Davis, take that Apache down to Obie's hangar."

"Sure, Skipper." I leaped to my feet and was heading for the door when he called me back, "Don't bother - you will never manage to start it."

"Sure I will Skipper." I was hugely offended. I may not have been much of a pilot, but I had a good understanding of machinery. Hell, I had raced and maintained my own cars and motorbikes. In fact, I had recently modified my MG TA to take a Roots supercharger. What could be so difficult about starting a perfectly ordinary aeroplane?

"Okay, let's put it this way," Zingi sneered, "If you can start it you can taxi it."

You may be wondering why I was so desperate to taxi this magnificent aeroplane. The truth is that I had never sat in the left hand seat of any twin in my entire life. So to taxi one would be a massive treat for me. I could visualise myself waiving casually to Sculk Barnard as I taxied past his control tower.

To keep this story short, I have to admit that after spending about an hour fiddling with every knob and switch I could find in the aeroplane I was still no closer to finding the starters. Zingi came out and showed me where the buttons were. They were hidden, out of sight, under the left hand side of the instrument panel. Bastard!

Anyhow, on with the story of how I came close to death in Bertie's brown and white 235 Apache. This was just before he bought it.

I was almost wetting myself with excitement at the thought of riding in such a splendid aeroplane. Zingi had pushed me through the luggage door into the boot. Jack Jay, our new wonder-boy from England, was converting to his first twin. My duty was to help getting it up to gross weight as the bristly little Major Bomb-doors Pidsley was putting the finishing touches to Jack's conversion.

Jack and Bomb-doors were in the front, Zingi and Gerald Kroak, from the workshops, occupied the middle row, and I was in the single seat in the boot. No matter, I was in an aeroplane – and that's all that counted. Our mission was to do three full-load landings.

The first two were great. The trouble started on the downwind leg for our third, and final, landing. Bomb-doors decided to simulate an engine failure on the left engine. Yes, that's the one with the hydraulic pump that powers the gear and flaps. All went well while Bomb-doors and Jack busied themselves with checklists, feathering props, messing with levers and then a final frenzied yanking up and down of the "donkey's-dong". This was an emergency, red-handled hydraulic-pump that was used to build up pressure to get the gear and flaps down.

The trouble was they were so busy with their heads in the cockpit that they allowed the downwind leg to converge towards the field. Twin pilots who are reading this are now beginning to squirm in their seats - they can see where this was going. And they are quite right. We had almost no base leg, and Jack did a classic trick - he overshot the centreline, forcing us to do a hammerhead. This called for a steep turn - into the dead engine, at low airspeed.

Although I didn't know it at the time, we were in an extremely precarious position. We could do the steep turn and risk spinning in. Heavy twins, turning into the dead engine, with everything hanging out, and the airspeed bleeding off, are prone to inverting themselves.

Our only other option was to try for a gentle turn, and do a go-around. But heavy twins don't like going around on one engine. They particularly don't like it up-country, with the gear and flaps hanging out. Even if Jack and the major pumped like hell and managed to get the gear and flaps up before we hit the ground there was still little chance of climbing away unless they managed to start the dead engine while struggling with the hydraulics. There just wasn't time for everything.

As I said, we were in serious trouble. So serious, in fact, that the aircraft started to shudder.

By looking between all the intervening shoulders I could just see the ASI with 85 mph showing, so I knew we couldn't be stalling. I assumed the shudder was something to do with the feathered prop.

It was only later, when I asked Zingi about it, that I understood we were on the verge of stalling and spinning in. I asked how that could happen at 85 mph when the aircraft normally stalled at about 60 mph. Zingi just said, "Bugger off and do some reading".

So that was the second time that the gentle Clark-Y wing section saved my life.

It was also the day that Zingi put one more survival tool in my bucket. I was unbelievably lucky to have Zingi and Old Piet as my mentors during the phase when many folks kill themselves.

I still had less than 100 hours in my logbook.

* * *

Bombdoors & Guti

The day after my Lobatse flight with Zingi, I had one of the most terrifying flights of my life.

Zingi had briefed Bomb-doors and I to go to Salisbury (now Harare) via Pietersburg to pick up a passenger. We did this and then headed for Salisbury.

I was flying the 235 Cherokee from the left hand seat because we were using this flight as part of my conversion. So Bomb-doors was PIC in the right hand seat.

As we approached the Limpopo we realised there was a solid bank of low cloud ahead. It stretched as far as we could see to the east, but we thought it might break up towards the west, so we headed that way. There was no over-or-under decision - Bomb-doors didn't have a current instrument rating. So we descended to get underneath the muck.

When I say the word 'guti' there is a sucking in of breath from all who know this special from of Zimbo weather. It is caused by an influx of cold air from the Indian Ocean, and is most common around mid-summer. It produces low cloud and drizzle that can hang around for days.

Anyhow, neither of us knew enough to suck in our breath - we simply descended below it while heading further west - to avoid the worst of it.

I hear another sucking of breath by those who know Zim and its famous Matobo hills. These are not so much hills but a scattering of massive Ayers Rock-like boulders that rise almost vertically out of the landscape.

If you now combine the Matobo boulders, a layer of guti covering their tops, a light aircraft, and a misty drizzle whose drops are too small to blow off the windscreen of said aircraft, you will understand the sucking of breath - much of which was now coming from inside the aeroplane.

It was a truly terrifying experience because we only saw the boulders in transit - as they passed our side-windows. We had no idea what lay ahead. There was no time to waste, we were about to become strawberry jam on a cliff-face.

Although I was flying, I was technically not in charge, but I felt the need to get the Major to climb us out of this mess. He refused, saying that his rating was not current, and besides he was in the right hand seat and couldn't see the instruments properly.

When you are about to merge with the vertical scenery, there is very little time for discussions, so I am afraid I did a Mutiny on the Bounty thing. I had spotted a mielie field about the size of a tennis court on my side. I told the Major either he took the controls and climbed through the guti immediately, or I would land in the mielies.

This got his attention. He took full power, hauled the nose up and leaned across my side to see the instruments.

For a paralysing period of time we sat in the muck wondering whether we would take our last breath as a black wall loomed a few feet in front of the windscreen.

It seemed like half an hour, but it was probably only a few minutes before we popped out of the top in dazzling sunshine.

I don't think the Major and I said a single word to each other. I flew us to Salisbury and landed at Mount Hamden in complete silence. We never mentioned this flight again. I know neither of us was proud of the way we had conducted ourselves, both getting into the guti and getting out of it. We knew it was nothing but brute luck that saved our lives that day.

* * *

My logbook says that the next day I ferried a Tri-Pacer, VP-YVF from Mount Hamden to Beit Bridge. It took 3h 15m and I have no idea what that was about. But it shows that either we simply ignored the regs, or no one bothered to enforce them, because I have never held a Zim licence and therefore had no right to be flying this aeroplane.

Strangely, the following day I flew a Tri-Pacer, ZS-CKL from Beit Bridge to Wonderboom. I can't help feeling that it was the same aeroplane - just travelling incognito.

Actually over the next two days I flew it all over the Reef and to several places in the Free State, and eventually left it at the magnificent Westminster estate, 60 nautical miles due east of Bloemfontein.

Zingi had told me to take it there to show to a Lord Elpus (or some such name). I phoned the gentleman to make final arrangements for my visit. His butler answered and said he would find out whether his lordship was in. I could then hear his voice echoing through the mighty building as he explained that there appeared to be an aeroplane salesman wishing to converse with the master of the estate.

Eventually his lordship picked up the instrument with a cautious "Hellair?"

We soon made arrangements for me to arrive there around noon the next day. I wanted to be very sure that I would find his farm strip. "Oh it's terribly easy, old boy. It's a green strip of grass slap in between two wheat fields. You can't possibly miss it. And I'll collect you in the old Land-Rover, what."

Anyone who has flown over that part of the Free-State at harvesting time will have spotted my problem already. The whole damn country consists of wheat fields separated by strips of green grass. I picked the most likely looking strip and landed there. It seemed more like an overgrown track for farm machinery. I waited around for a while, but no Land-Rovers hove into sight, so I took off again and mooched around the sky looking for a more likely spot – none presented itself.

However I eventually observed a gentleman driving a huge green harvesting machine through the wheat. I landed behind him and enquired about the whereabouts of the Lord Elpus aerodrome. He pointed to a cluster of trees and a riverbed less than a mile away. I went and circled that area until I spotted a green bit that might just be considered to be a crop-spraying strip. Mistake, I went through two fairly substantial ditches, hidden by the grass, before bringing the Trike to a stop.

A local appeared out of the undergrowth and explained that his lordship was waiting for me in the adjacent field.

I braved the two ditches again, hopped over the fence and there was the Land-Rover, together with a tweed-clad Peer who waved encouragingly.

I finally landed on a chunk of territory that was not noticeable better than my three previous alighting spots. Hardly had the propeller stopped turning than he wrenched the door open. Stuck a lordly hand in to shake mine and greet me with the words, "I'll take it – just what I need, old chap, something that will land anywhere."

I phoned Zingi and told him I had just completed my first sale. I suppose I had hoped for some words of congratulation, but all I got was, "Well get on the train. And make it second-class."

* * *

Very soon after that I had another nonsense with the Tri-Pacer. Zingi had told me to retrieve one from Rand airport. He had made no secret of the fact that it was seriously urgent.

Someone dropped me off there and I legged round to the hangar. As is so often the case when you are in a hurry, fate is not on your side. This miserable looking blue and white aeroplane was sitting right at the back of the hangar. It had a flat tire, and had made itself home to a large number of spiders.

Now, I am not hopelessly arachnophobic, but close. Put it this way: if one parashot on to my lap during takeoff there would certainly be a nasty accident. I have this picture of mangled aeroplane, broken bones protruding through flesh, and perhaps a piece of spleen waggling slightly as the wind gently rocks the aircraft. The offending spider may just be glimpsed, scuttling into a dark part of the broken fuselage.

All of which means it was necessary to enlist the assistance of helpers to pump the tyre, move a dozen aeroplanes, and vacuum the web-builders from all parts of the cabin.

It is fortunate that cell-phones were not part of one's life in those days as I was able to visualize Zingi blowing a gasket when I was not back at headquarters within a couple of hours of his ETA for me.

But things were still to get worse. There was a further delay when I found the battery to be dead flat. Jump leads were produced, and after a bit of chugging and churning the machinery spluttered into fairly unenthusiastic life.

Those of you familiar with Rand airport will recall that it is all uphill to the threshold of 29, and thereafter all downhill. This geographic formation was to feature prominently in the events which were to follow.

The uphill taxi meant that I had no call to use the brakes, also there was no reason to stop at the threshold as the tower had given me takeoff clearance en-route. I decided to dispense with pre-takeoff formalities due to the pressing nature of my mission. As we screeched on to the runway I moved the throttle all the way forward.

Now, Tri-pacers came in four flavours, some had 125HP, others 135HP then there was the mighty 150HP version and finally the startling 160HP one. I had been in such a hurry that I had no idea which this was, however its response to full throttle made me realize that this example didn't fall into any of the above categories.

Acceleration could best be described as noticeable. I juggled with the carb-heat and mixture, but nothing made much difference. It soon became obvious that this specific Tri-Pacer had an affinity for the planet. I decided to let it have its way, so I throttled fully back and yanked hard on the donkey's-prick handbrake, with a red knob on the end, which hung below the centre of the panel.

I needn't have bothered – it did nothing at all.

Obviously, if I had done a run-up I would have discovered both the lack of going, and lack of stopping, power, at the same time.

What saved my bacon was my previous tailwheel flying, where one quickly got used to shedding speed by ducking on to the grass, between flare-path lights, and then ground-looping, or turning uphill, or into wind.

I am a slow learner. This happened in February 1964 and

although it gave me pause to consider the value of pre-takeoff checks, it wasn't until a year later, in February 1965 when a Twin Comanche took me by the generals and demanded that I do things properly, or it would wrap me in a fireball in the desert sand.

I will tell you about that when we get there

* * *

During the next three days I logged 20 hrs and 15 minutes with Old Piet, in 235 Cherokee, ZS-DUE, flying through South Africa, Swaziland and Mozambique. Here are some of the places we visited, Komatipoort, Lourenco Marques, Beira, Quelimane, Petersburg, Mica, Stegi and Manzini.

I mention this for a few of reasons. First, it put hours in my logbook very quickly. Second, I saw a hell of a lot of Southern Africa. And third, much as Old Piet's flying left a lot to be desired - I was still able to learn a great deal on these flights.

Furthermore my bladder control was put to the test on the longer of these journeys. On one occasion an even newer boy than me, Don Rotherow, was delegated to fly with the boss.

Don, either didn't plan, or simply couldn't take the strain, but on a the long Quelimane to Wonderboom leg, more than 800 nautical miles, things got out of hand.

"Mr. Piet, we need to land."

"I don't sink so."

"But I have got to have a weewee."

"So vare do you sink I should land?" Said Mr. Piet, waiving his arm generously round the scenery, to indicate a massive expanse of nowhere to land. "Here, use zis." he said, after digging in various pockets and eventually pulling out a pair of earphones, wrapped in a plastic bag.

Don extracted the phones and viewed the bag with suspicion. Eventually he decided it would do the trick so he started squirming sideways to conceal the deed from his boss. After a while he confessed that he couldn't do it there, declaring that he felt the back seat might make a more suitable venue for the proposed decanting.

He clambered into the back and was eventually successful.

Now, those of you who have flown Piper singles will remember that they only have a storm window on the left, which meant that in order to dispose of the plastic bag of yellow liquid, it had to be passed in front of the pilot's face and pushed out through an opening a little bigger than the palm of your hand.

It is not recorded exactly how the floppiness of the bag, combined with the rushing of wind, conspired to distribute the entire contents of the pouch on Mr. Piet's face and shirtfront - but that's what happened.

When they landed at Wonderboom, an hour later, Old Piet emerged from the aircraft wiping his face and his upper body with his battered brown hat.

"Zingi," he said, "last week you employed zis bastard, and today he pisses all over me. I sink I prefer to fly with zat moron Davis."

Thus my job was once again secure - at least until my next misdemeanour.

* * *

Folks Coming Second

At this stage, my logbook has a photo of a leggy young lady, with considerable frontal talent and negligible clothing, reclining on the wing of a Cherokee. In fact I remember the occasion well. The aircraft, ZS-DVC had spent some days in Obie's workshop having a glass panel put in the floor.

The owner, an excitable and demanding Pole named Max Kolb, had wanted this done so that his new aeroplane would be suitable for aerial photography. He was, in fact, a hugely respected fashion photographer from Durban. I am not really sure how the glass floor would benefit his career, but who am I to question such things? I remember him having fits of artistic temperament that even intimidated Zingi.

"Max is coming at ten o'clock to collect his aeroplane, so you just stay out of sight. I don't want you stuffing up the deal."

Anyhow, he collected his aeroplane without any temper tantrums and set sail for Durban. We never heard from him again - however we did hear *about* him.

It seems that, about a year later, Jerry Stegi, our Piper dealer and maintenance guy in Durban, got an excited call from a lady, perhaps the one in the picture, saying that she had had a row with Max and he was on his way out to Virginia Airfield to kill himself in the aeroplane. She wanted Jerry to disable the aircraft to prevent this disaster.

Now, this put Jerry in a hell of a difficult position. Not only did he hanger Max's aircraft, he also did all the maintenance. It was hardly his place to render his customer's aircraft unserviceable on the say-so of an hysterical female. However he also realized the implications of ignoring the request.

Eventually Jerry compromised - he let the air out of one of

the main oleos. No pilot in his right mind could fail to notice this, so he would naturally come to Jerry and ask for it to be fixed. Then Jerry could take his time and hope his customer calmed down.

Well this was not to be. Max dragged his lopsided aircraft out of the hangar, leaped aboard and was soon taxying out for a 'local flight'.

He got airborne and turned straight out to sea. Durban picked him up on radar and enquired about his intentions. They got more than they had bargained for. He told them of his tangled love-life and how he was going to commit his earthly being to the depths of the Indian Ocean. Soon he was out of VHF range, but thoughtfully continued on HF. After about two and a half hours of this (the aeroplane had around 5 hours endurance) Max asked ATC to say goodbye to the world and particularly to his mother and his girlfriend. After which nothing more was heard of him.

Very sad, you might say, however the story doesn't end there. About a year later a fishing trawler operating a couple of miles off the coast, and some distance north of Durban, snagged something in it's net. After much heaving and struggling, up came Max's Cherokee - pretty much intact – it certainly hadn't been dived into the sea.

As far as I remember there was no body in it. It would seem that Max chickened out, got below the radar and sneaked back, running out of fuel just before reaching the coast.

Conspiracy theorists speculated about the possibility of his going to make a new life for himself in Mozambique. Possible, but I think unlikely.

* * *

Because other people's flights obviously don't feature in my logbooks, it is difficult to put exact dates to them, however it was about this time - mid 1964. That Jack Jay, the guy who nearly spun us into the ground during his Apache conversion with Bomb-doors, did himself in, in Angola.

We had sold a 235 Cherokee to a mining company whose head office was in Luanda. Jack flew the aircraft up there and was met by three of their directors. It seems they wanted him to deliver the aircraft to the mine, somewhere inland. They also thought it would be a brilliant idea if Jack was to do a fly-past while a photographer filmed the event.

So Jack and the three directors climbed aboard, took off, did a 180 and dived down on the man with the cine-camera, which was mounted on a solid tripod. Looking through the viewfinder, the photographer didn't have the correct perspective of how fast and low the aircraft was.

Perhaps it was the heavy load, or the high temperature, or simply a desire to push things to the limit. Whatever the reason, Jack managed to take the photographer's head off with the wing. A very nasty business.

But it immediately became a whole lot more nasty. The massive camera sliced through the bottom skin of the wing. Jack obviously got a hell of a fright and hauled back on the pole. The G forces, combined with the weakened wing structure caused the wing to fold upwards and the whole lot went into the ground upside-down. There were no survivors.

In fact Placo barely survived. We were sued by the company, or the insurers, or someone, because our pilot had caused this devastation. I don't remember the amount, but it was certainly enough to close us down.

Ultimately we were able to show that our contract was to deliver the aircraft to Luanda, and that Jack was acting on his own when he agreed to fly it on to the mine.

* * *

Another disaster occurred around this time. Placo had recently employed Quinton Posthumus, a handsome young pilot, with very little experience.

Anyhow he was dispatched to Cape Town in a 140 Cherokee to use his charm to rustle up some business and sell a few aeroplanes. The target market was the flying clubs and schools. We were deliberately selling 140 Cherokees at exactly the same price as 150 Cessnas in order to corner the training market. This would soon lead to Piper-trained pilots wanting to buy Pipers rather than Cessnas. The strategy worked extremely well - world wide.

In those days, Youngsfield was still in operation. It was at Kennilworth, in the shadow of Table Mountain. It was a wonderful old-time genuine airfield - no runways - just a big squarish grass field, which meant that you never had to cope with crosswinds.

Exactly how Quentin hoped to justify flying-school sales, by taking three young ladies for a ride in a 140 Cherokee, is not recorded.

The first we heard was a phone call to Zingi, saying that the aircraft had crashed killing all on board.

It turned out to be the old story - the one that had nearly put an end to Erick and I. A beat-up, followed by a stall-turnish thing that went wrong. And they spun into the ground.

Again, Placo was left to prove that Jack was acting in his own interests and not as a representative of the company.

* * *

Then we had another death. A young guy named Wagner, I think, was delivering a Bonanza to Durban. Weather forced him down into a valley and he hit power lines. Fortunately he was alone.

This was a year for me to take careful note of the mistakes of others. Somehow one was becoming hardened to these deaths. Not that I was unaffected by their impact, but rather that I was able to analyse them and see them for what they were. God was not randomly swatting people out of the sky - they were all masters of their own destinies.

* * *

Then there was the very sad business of Ken Anders, who it turned out was not master of his own destiny.

Ken was one of those guys who is immaculate in all he did. He dressed immaculately, and he flew immaculately. Everything was just so, and by the book, which is why his accident took us all by surprise.

Ken was flying a charter in a Twin Comanche. He was on his way to Bloemfontein at flight level 85 (roughly 4000 ft above ground level), when witnesses saw the aircraft put its nose down vertically and dive straight into the ground.

The cause of the accident was a huge mystery. The aircraft was almost new, and properly maintained. It was a crystal clear day, and Ken's reputation was unblemished. The DCA finally concluded that the windscreen must have broken and blown in, incapacitating the pilot. This was indeed a reasonable finding because there was an Airworthiness Directive out at the time, dealing with cracks round the edges of Twin Comanche windscreens.

So there the matter stood for something like two years. Then the investigation was suddenly re-opened. Here's what happened.

We employed a new salesman, Angus Mackenzie (we used to call him Fungus). He was there to replace Jack Jay or Quinten Posthumus or someone.

Fungus was a great floppy, awkward guy with arms like an orangutan. Zingi, who was a great mimic, would demonstrate how Fungus would react to being crapped on by Zingi – a fairly frequent occurrence. He would go even more floppy than usual, stand on one leg and throw his right hand over the top of his head to scratch his left ear. This had us all in fits.

Anyhow, to get on with the story, Fungus returned from somewhere, in a Twin Comanche. Afternoon thunderstorms had built up and Fungus had managed to get on the wrong side of one of these Charlie Bravos which spat substantial lumps of hail at him.

The pilot's windscreen broke around the edges and the whole thing came on him. Actually that's not quite true, it didn't come on him. It simply came in a few inches and stayed there. The pressure in the cabin must have equalled that of the outside air, and no one was any the worse for the event.

When Fungus was telling us about it, with great animation and excitement, he also declared that he had been struck by lightning.

Zingi's comment was, "Yes, we all know that, Fungus. But when?".

Anyhow, in the light of this event, the CAA had another look at Ken Anders' crash, and came to a horrifying conclusion. It seems his passenger, whose name I have forgotten, had a motor dealership in Bloem. The finances were not good, and nor was his marriage, but he had substantial life insurance. He was a big man and would have had no problem overpowering the immaculate, but small framed Ken.

I still get the horrors when I think about that. I have only once had to struggle with a guy in a cockpit, and it is, to me, the most scary thing that can happen to a pilot.

While we are on the subject of death and misery there were three more accidents at around that time.

The first was a fellow named Henry Hunt who was the managing director of Williams Hunt, the General Motors dealership that owned the Beech franchise at the time.

He was demonstrating a Beech Musketeer at Wonderboom. There were three species of Musketeer – they came with horsepowers of 150, 180 and 200. They should have been good aircraft. They were exceptionally well built, roomy, comfortable and solid. Unfortunately it was their build quality and solidness that let them down, because it made them very heavy. Even the 200HP model had anaemic performance, and the other two were barely up to taxying.

As far as I remember Henry was flying the mighty 200HP version. So impressed was he by all that power that he thought he would use it to impress the passengers, and us spectators, with a stall-turn/wingover type of thing, with four up.

Neither the aeroplane nor the pilot were up to that sort of thing and so four people died in front of our eyes.

Unbelievably, the next year, at an airshow, not at Wonderboom this time, the Company's new CEO, whose name I have forgotten, and three passengers did exactly the same thing, but in a Bonanza this time. Again, killing all on board.

Finally, Fungus Mackenzie did an almost identical thing at Parys in another Beechcraft – I think it was a Baron this time.

* * *

And to finish off this morbid chapter, we lost another salesman, whose name I have forgotten – actually I think he just acted for us – part time.

Anyhow he had a customer who had just bought a single Comanche. He and the customer, plus two young ladies set sail for Lourenco Marques (now Maputo) for the weekend. They flew into cloud, without instrument ratings, lost it and spiralled into the ground, killing all on board.

Again, the rellies of the deceased decided to go for Placo to compensate them for their losses. The fact that the buyer had already bought the aircraft and the purpose of the trip was a dirty weekend at the coast rather spoiled their chances of screwing Placo.

The court case was very interesting. It was held in Pretoria and presided over by Judge Cecil Margo, of Helderburg fame. Cecil, I think held a commercial pilot licence and was an active flyer – he knew about light aircraft.

The prosecution were trying to show that Placo's pilot was in the left hand seat, and was therefore PIC. With this objective they got Zingi into the witness box – a bad mistake as it turns out.

Prosecution: Mr. Harrison did you witness the deceased boarding the aircraft?

Zingi: Yes I did

Prosecution: Perhaps you could tell the court who was the first to enter the aircraft.

Zingi: Certainly. It was one of the young ladies.

Prosecution: And which door did she enter through?

Zingi: The right-hand door.

Zingi glances at Cecil Margo and, for a moment, they exchange a fleeting smile. They both know where this cross-examination is heading.

The prosecution then leads Zingi, step by step, through the sequence of who entered the aeroplane in what order and through which door. Of course they had all entered through the right hand door.

Finally the prosecutor reaches his moment of triumph – the point where he thrusts his sword through Zingi, and proves that Placo's pilot was in the left hand seat. Obviously Zingi has had everyone entering through the right hand door – there is no other.

Prosecutor: Mr. Harrison, are you asking this court to believe that in order to fly the aircraft my client scrambled over the other occupants so as to get into the pilot's seat. Surely, if he was flying, he would simply have entered from the other side.

Zingi: No, sir, the aircraft only has one door.

Prosecutor: Splutter, gurgle, um, ah. Right. Now let's proceed to my next point.

Cecil Margo pulls out a white handkerchief and makes a big thing of blowing his nose. Zingi turns away and has a coughing fit into his sleeve. Both are trying to hide their mirth.

* * *

Neville

Many of the characters I have discussed so far have been transitory in my life – either because our paths only crossed for a short while, or because they were killed. But every now and then you bump into someone who becomes a lifelong friend.

I was in the middle of some important duty in the hangar when my domain was intruded upon by a figure who, at first glance, appeared to be a scarecrow. He was an extremely skinny and washed-out looking human being of about 30. He had a beakish nose, tatty khaki shorts and a paint splattered shirt that was now well past its toss-by date.

He wore no shoes and his hair mostly stood on end. On closer examination, his hands were ingrained with filth and his finger nails looked as if he had used them for tunnelling.

Not being the neatest character myself I felt something in the nature of a bond, or rapport, with the intruder.

"May I help you, sir?" I asked.

"I'm thinking of buying an aerie, so I thought I would just have a look round."

"Certainly, sir. Will you be using it for...?" I heard the dreaded clatter of the window between Zingi's office and the hangar opening.

"Davis." He bellowed.

"Excuse me, sir," I said to my potential customer, and bolted across the hangar ducking between aeroplanes.

Zingi beckoned me closer so that he didn't need to raise his voice. He had the look of a diner who has found a gecko in his soup. "Get that fucking tramp out of my hangar."

"No, Skipper, it's fine. He wants to buy an aeroplane."

"Come closer, Davis," said Zingi, adjusting his bow-tie, and speaking very slowly and quietly. "I don't like repeating myself. Now get that fucking tramp out of my hangar. Im-med-iate-ly."

I gave Zingi what I hoped was a look of disdainful reproach. Then turned and tripped over a tow-bar. My look was wasted, he had already shut the window and forgotten about me.

"Why don't we go and look at some of these aeries outside?" I invited the scarecrow. We looked at, and discussed, several aircraft on the grass, and when it seemed that he would like to return to the hangar I invited him into my house, which was just 50 yards away, for a cup of tea.

He turned out to be Neville Austin, the famous racing driver, who raced the only D-Type Jag in the country. He was a contemporary, and friend, of Tony Maggs, who many will remember for his Formula-one racing. Neville was far too modest to volunteer all this information – I had to wheedle it out of him.

He was obviously well-educated and turned out to be the chief design engineer for Asea – a company that built massive gantry cranes. Neville was, and still is, extremely bright.

We got on splendidly, and he genuinely wanted to buy an aircraft. He particularly had his eye on a Colt, ZS-CTF. This would be his first aeroplane as he had only just got his licence.

My problem was to demonstrate the aircraft without Zingi spotting us. It actually turned out to be quite easy. I suggested Neville collect his wife, Barbara, and return the next day at lunch time, when I knew Zingi would not be around.

All went according to plan. We bundled Barbara into the boot. Takeoff was on runway 11 and we turned out left to go and fly over Neville's farm, Haakdoornboom. We may have even landed there – I don't remember.

However I do remember the abuse that Zingi hurled at me when we returned. He appeared out of the shadows and stood in front of the hangar with hands on hips.

You know when people speak very quietly, and you have to move closer to hear what they are saying. Then they bellow in your face. Army Drill-Sergeants have perfected this technique over many years. In fact, had the military been on a recruiting drive for such personnel they couldn't have done better than to interview Zingi.

He enquired what I knew about weight-and-balance. My hang-jaw expression told him, correctly, that I had never heard the term before.

He waited till Neville and Barbara had left. I suspect they saw that they might be caught in the cross-fire from Zingi's tirade. He then grabbed me by the ear, walked me to the aircraft, shoved my head inside and asked me to count the seats. I knew I could get this one right.

"Two," I replied.

"And seat-belts?"

"Two sets, Skipper." This was easy.

"So how many people do you think it is insured to carry?"

"Again, two." Obviously. Duh

"And what does that label say about the maximum load in the back of the aircraft?"

"100 lbs." This was really easy.

"So what do you suppose would happen to Placo if you killed the tramp and his trouble and strife? And their families sued us."

"Ah, now you have got me, Skipper, I am not well up on legal matters."

"Well I am, Davis, we would be out of business. You are fired."

I let him cool off overnight. In the morning I brought him a signed purchase order for the Colt. It was the very first aeroplane I ever sold.

Zingi viewed me coldly and eventually said, "Fuck off into the hangar and make me some tea." So I guessed this meant that I had been unfired. Again.

* * *

At about this time I became addicted to spinning Cubs. Obviously it was double the fun if you could find someone else who was enthusiastic about being spun, and who might even pay for the privilege. Nobody took any notice of illegal charters in those days – unless you bought a Dak and set up in opposition to Comair or NAC.

I offered Neville the privilege of coming with me for a spin in a J3 Cub, but he was strangely unenthusiastic. Neville had been round the block a couple of times in the motor racing world, and knew the penalties for showing off.

Strangely, although they had a happy marriage, Neville had no objection to Barbara coming along. I think she was the only passenger I have ever had who couldn't get enough of spinning. She loved it and screeched with delight every time the little yellow aeroplane rolled, half inverted, into the spin, with a loud clonk from the left wing – where the attachment bolt-holes had been worn oval.

* * *

Neville seemed to attract trouble for me. For instance there was the time when Zingi told me to take a 235 Cherokee to Fort Victoria to demonstrate to the Parks Board.

I thought it would be a pity not to take my new-found friends with me, so I arranged to load them aboard at 6 am – long before Zingi came to work. The idea was to clear customs at Pietersburg but that turned out to be QBI (Q-Code meaning flight under IFR – Instrument Flight Rules - is compulsory, ie. the area was covered in very low cloud, obscuring visibility). But it was imperative that we get away smartly before being spotted so we set sail for Potgietersrust and waited there until Pietersburg gave us Special VFR below. We snuck in, cleared Customs and Immigration and set sail for Fort Vic.

We spent two nights in the hotel there, did the demo flights, and the next morning headed for Hippo Valley Sugar Estate where Neville had to inspect two of the massive gantry cranes that he had sold to them.

The trouble started when I landed back at headquarters, a day later than expected. I had dropped Neville and Barbara off on their farm, after clearing in at Pietersburg again.

When I landed, I noticed Zingi striding towards the aircraft, with the air of one who has a compelling mission to undertake. Perhaps, after my successful tour of the Colonies he was going to send me off to some new and exciting destination – I was beginning to get a taste for this business of flying nice aeroplanes to exotic places.

As he got closer I noticed his face was set in something less than a welcoming attitude – in fact he looked bloody angry.

"Where the hell have you just come from?" he enquired.

"From Fort Vic, Skipper." I lied.

"Don't talk shit to a policeman." I could tell that he was really quite disturbed. An observation which he confirmed with a substantial monologue, touching on my general moronic demeanour and irresponsible conduct. He seemed to have a thing about Neville's relatives suing Placo into oblivion, should I inflict bodily injury, or death, on either Neville or Barbara.

It was one of those one-sided conversations that never seem to end. Zingi would stare at me in disgust before turning on his heel and heading back to the hangar. Then some new insight would enter his mind and he would stride back to me. "And another thing – what the hell do you think…?" And he would launch into further offensive one-sided dialogue on the subject of what might have happened if so-and-so.

This was beginning to become a bit tedious. I was trying to get my clobber out of the aeroplane and put it to bed, and Zingi kept following me around and yelling at me. I was becoming quite annoyed, and was trying to think of some snappy remark which would put him in his place.

However, I was beaten to it – he closed the discussion with the now familiar phrase, "Davis, you are bloody fired."

Well, how about that, I thought. Maybe I will teach the bastard a lesson, and just not come back. But in the end I forgave him and went into the hangar to help Hendrick, the other hangar-boy, with our cleaning and polishing duties.

* * *

Neville had a bunch of kids who were rapidly growing, so he soon realized he needed a bigger aeroplane. What could be more sensible that the flying milk-stool that Mr. Piper called a Tri-Pacer?

Neville located exactly what he wanted – it was a pranged one that was being rebuilt in Placo Workshops, under the watchful eye of the dreaded Obie Oberholzer.

I have to go off at a tangent here to tell you why he was the 'dreaded' Oberholzer. He was a massive, tough, extremely knowledgeable, and very organized German. The problem was that he bore a poorly-concealed grudge over the final scores of last two world wars, and the world cup. He almost seemed to hold me responsible for the fatherland's poor sporting and military performances.

In short, from the day I joined Placo, I was the British face of all that was evil and intolerable in the world. He hated me with a passion.

Zingi would say, "Davis, take that aeroplane down to Obie and tell him to fix it."

"Sure, Skipper." It would then be my massive privilege to taxi, say a 235 Cherokee, past Schalk Barnard, in his little wooden control tower, where I would give him a cheerful wave, which was generally ignored. I would then continue down past ISCOR's hangar and the Pretoria Flying Club in the hope of perhaps seeing Jan Hoenbos, the airport manager, who would also be graced with a look-at-me wave. Finally I would reach the hard-stand in front of Obie's hangar.

As soon as he spotted me he would storm out of the building. As the engine was wobbling its prop through the shut-down shudder, Obie would be bellowing at me to get that bloody aircraft off his concrete.

I would climb out on to the wing and look down on him with the cool contempt that comes from knowing I am following Zingi's orders, and am therefore bulletproof.

"Go on. Fuck off. Get out of here!" he would thunder.

"Zingi told me to bring this aeroplane for you to fix."

"Oh, I see – that's different," he would say with a sarcastic curl to his German lip, and a glint from his steel rimmed glasses. "And what do you suppose is exactly wrong with it?"

"How would I know?" I would retort, wondering why he thought Zingi would entrust me with such information.

"Well kindly tell Zingi I can't fix it if I don't know what the hell's wrong with it. Moron."

I would mutter darkly about bloody Germans, and the war, and sneak back to HQ, behind the hangars so that folks couldn't see me walking, when I was normally doing important things with aeroplanes.

Anyhow, back to the Trike that Obie was rebuilding for sale to Neville. In those days a Tri-Pacer represented a lot of money, so Neville had to sell his Colt before he could buy the Tri-Pacer. The problem was that Obie was quite capable of selling the Tri-Pacer to the first person to come with a handful of notes.

In the meantime Neville got Obie to paint the Trike a plain, no-lines-or-stripes, all-over nipple-pink. It looked bilious – it was disgusting. But I told you Neville is smart. He knew that he had eliminated all other potential buyers. No one in the world would want to own that aeroplane. Its registration was ZS-CSR but if was forever after known as Austin's flying tit.

I have no idea what eventually happened to it, but it served Neville well for 2000 hours – mainly into Botswana and the swamps. He finally replaced it with a 235 Cherokee – and after that a Twin Comanche and finally a Seneca, which I eventually bought for my flying school – but that was many years later.

In the meantime, Neville and Zingi had somehow become the best of friends. Neville had started Delta camp in the Okavango. And he and Zingi and both families would fly there whenever they got the chance.

While they were enjoying each other's company, I had fallen out with Zingi. I had sold a brand new 235 to Potgieter's Motors in Kimberley, and Zingi had come up behind me in the office while I was negotiating, on the phone, to fly for them.

Zingi hit the roof and told me to bugger off then, so I did just that. I went to Kimberley for three times the salary that Placo were paying me.

* * *

My next flying experience with Neville was when I bought my Tiger Moth, ZS-CNT (that non-U aeroplane, as one ATC rudely called it. Bad dog, Spot). I flew it up from Kimberley to show it off to Neville.

Now Neville's runway was seriously downhill. It was little more than a dirt track running away from the house, between two mielie fields to 'T' into a cross-runway, of similar quality – also surrounded by mielies.

I landed up-hill, because that's part of the deal in a Tiger with no brakes. By the time we had finished chatting and it was time to take Neville flying in my magic machine, quite a serious crosswind had sprung up, so I elected to taxi down the one runway in order to use the cross one for takeoff.

Being a very inexperienced Tiger pilot I let the brute get away from me while taxying downhill. There wasn't sufficient width, between the mielies, to do a 180.

I bellowed at Neville to leap out and restrain the beast, but he was too smart for that. He would have been zapped by the tailplane and rolled in the dust.

In the end, we bounced across the bottom runway and straight into a mielie-field. I didn't even have the sense to stop the engine. So we sat there while the prop lazily flung mielies into the air on either side.

Neville never shared my enthusiasm for Tigers. He claimed that they were held together by the termites holding hands. He also criticised them for the fact that the only time the slip-needle (equivalent of the ball) was ever in the middle was when it was in transit to the other side. Of course this was a design fault of the Tiger, and nothing to do with the fact that Neville had never learned to use his feet.

Despite this shortcoming, Neville has remained one of my greatest friends for over 50 years. He was also huge buddies with Zingi until he died.

* * *

One quick, last story about Neville. He was on his way to Cape Town in his pink Tri-Pacer when the engine developed a screeching noise and filled the cabin with smoke. In fact he was in the middle of a chat with Cape Town Information when this happened. His call went as follows.

"Information this is Charlie Sierra Romeo passing Worcester at flight level... EFFING HELL..."

There were no further comms as Neville dropped the mike and did a very neat forced landing at Worcester. The problem was a seized generator, which had caused the drive belt to catch fire.

It wasn't long before the local constabulary arrived saying that ATC told them of a Mayday call. Neville, of course, denied making a Mayday call, but one can't help having some admiration for Cape Town using a little poetic license in the interpretation of Neville's words.

* * *

Neville eventually closed his logbook with about 9000 total time – of which around 4000 were instructing. He was CFT at both the Pretoria Flying Club and the Maun Flying Club, and taught all four of his sons to fly in his Cub ZS-AYX. One of them, Johnnie, "borrowed" the aeroplane, and, for his first solo, took his aunt, Rose, for a few circuits and bumps on the farm strip. He was 15!

* * *

Scary Stuff Both Ways

I was walking along the verandah past Zingi's office when he called me in.

"Davis, you see that blue Tri-Pacer that is sitting in front of the hangar? Well take it down to Jerry Stegi in Durban, and he has got a Colt for you to bring back."

"Sure thing, Skipper." I am half way out the door in my enthusiasm to get going, when Zingi calls me back.

"Don't worry, you'll probably get bloody lost. I'll get Lombard to do it."

"Excuse me, Skipper – I have just been to Rhodesia and back without getting lost." Really, sometimes Zingi could be very irritating.

"Yes, and look how you stuffed that up – taking that tramp, Austin, with you."

"Ah, come on, Skipper, I really want to go. I have never been to Durban."

"That's exactly what I'm worried about." He paused and viewed me as if I were something he found stuck to the sole of his shoe after visiting the SPCA. "Davis." He started speaking very slowly and quietly, "If you stuff this up I will make it my personal business to see that you never get another flying job in your whole life. Do you understand me?"

"Wow, gee, thanks, Skipper." He shook his head sadly and turned back to his paperwork.

So off I go, and as usual Zingi is right. Everything goes pretty well until I am about half an hour out of Durban, when I suddenly decide I am lost. The confluence of two small rivers on the map, doesn't quite seem to tie up with what I can see below me.

This throws me into a mild panic. If I get lost I will never be allowed to fly again. Just when I am beginning to think it would be better to shoot myself in the head, I spot a little village. Better still, the main store has a red roof with the name of the village painted on it in white.

I put on carb-heat, pull the power back and stand the little aeroplane on its ear while I circle down, keeping the red roof in sight all the way. I even remember to warm up the engine a couple of times on the way down.

The writing on the roof tells me the place seems to be called Jokotea. But I will go a bit lower just to make sure. When I say a bit lower, I mean that my next 360 brings me down to tree-top level as I fly along the main street. Actually it is the only street.

I see there is another name on the front of the building. It seems to be one of those Afrikaans places with a double name – this one is called Algemene Handelaar. I will find it on my map when I get a bit of height. I will be easy to remember because it is sort of like Algernon Handlebar.

As I climb away to check my map the engine stops stone dead. No cough or splutter or any other form of apology. Just silence.

Naturally I am stunned, just three hundred feet up, in a sort of valley. I won't bore you with details of my mental state, or my desperate attempts to reignite the fire. Sufficient to say that prior to my confusion concerning our whereabouts, I had been preparing to run one tank dry. Naturally I had forgotten about this when I decided to dive-bomb the settlement in order to sort out my navigational ineptitude. So the thing had bitten me in the bum when I least expected it.

The short story is that the penny dropped and I changed tanks with immediate, and very satisfying results.

My navigation was not so easily resolved. I was unable to find either name on my map. Subsequently I found that many villages are called Jokotea – actually Joko Tea. And that the handlebar thing really means General Dealer. Both equally useless lumps of information for pinpointing one's position.

Fortunately, I had read Earnest Gann's "Fate is the Hunter", also the writings of Sir Francis Chichester about his attempted circumnavigation of the world in his, Gipsy Moth. Both these gentlemen recommended that when one is confused about the location of some geographic feature which happens to be perched on a line-feature, such as a river, railway or coastline, one should deliberately head to one side, and upon reaching the line one simply turns the other way until the delinquent attraction appears on the nose.

And so it was with Durban. I headed left until I hit the beach and then turned right and followed it. Sure enough, those knowledgeable gentlemen proved to be correct – Virginia airport appeared slap in front of me. How could it not?.

I have since learned that on such trips one should not be disturbed if minute locations don't seem to tie up with your World Aeronautical 1:1,000,000 Chart. If you ignore these minor problems they simply go away. However, I have found that what one must do is always keep the big picture in perspective. I am thinking of mountains, railways, coastlines and so on. If they are where they should be, then you are not lost. Being lost is more a mental ailment, rather than a physical one.

While on the subject I am of the school that believe a GPS is a backup to a paper map – not the other way round. But that is a story for another day.

I handed over the Tri-Pacer to Jerry, who had a maintenance setup at Virginia. And slept on a sofa in the Durban Wings Club – a rather stuffy mob who would have disapproved strongly, had they known.

It would give me great pleasure to report that the next day my flight back to Wonderboom in the Colt was less dramatic, but if I did, it would be a lie. If anything the return flight contained even more drama that the outbound one.

This was the end of January 1964 – smack in the middle of thunderstorm season. Those who are familiar with flying weather in South Africa will know that the Natal midlands can produce some of the most murderous flying conditions in the world. It is not that the weather is particularly worse than anywhere else – it is just that it moves, changes and develops unbelievably quickly. That area has more broken aeroplanes per square inch than anywhere else in Southern Africa.

Unfortunately, I quickly found out that it made no exceptions for rookies.

I can't be sure exactly where I was, but I think it was around Dundee. The reason for my doubt is that I had been foolish enough to get on top of cloud. At first there were gaps between the small, fair-weather cumulus clouds. But soon the gaps became less frequent, and then the clouds were holding hands, with only the odd hole between them.

When this happens you always think there is a big hole just past the next little ridge of cloud. So you keep going. Finally there are no more holes and it seems such a waste to go back and look for the last hole you saw. The truth is it has probably closed up by now in any case.

At the time none of this worried me in the least – I had yet to learn that when you play games with the weather, you are always the looser. I knew that the ground was rising beneath the cloud, so I thought it only reasonable that the cloud-tops were rising with it – and that's why they were getting closer to the aeroplane. Obviously the only thing was to climb.

Soon I began to realise that climbing didn't really seem to be doing the trick. The damn clouds never seemed to be far below the wheels.

I had started off at flight level 85, then climbed to 105. The little aeroplane was running out of breath as I tried to persuade her that 125 would be desirable. The tops of the clouds had that sharply defined cauliflower appearance.

You know when ordinary people look at clouds, they never seem to be doing much. They don't rush around – they have a sort of bovine inertia. If you look at a cloud, and then look back at it five minutes later – nothing has really changed.

Well actually that is all nonsense, and this was my day for learning that a developing cumulus grows vertically at a staggering rate which can easily out-climb jet airliners – so what hope does one have in a little 108 hp Colt?

Soon it seemed that the aeroplane's wheels were dragging in the cloud. Surely I should be able to climb faster than a silly cloud.

I made sure I had full power and leaned out further to speed us into the thinner atmosphere. Then checked the airspeed. I couldn't believe what I saw – it was showing 60 mph – I had been subconsciously pulling back on the stick. Obviously it was time to turn back. As I did so I realized the futility of the act – the clouds had built up all around me.

While I was pondering my options (none) the cloud simply enveloped me from below, and started buffeting me around.

At the time I had a total of 115 hrs and 45 minutes. Exactly 30 minutes of this had been instrument training. It must have been exceptionally good training because it gave me the confidence to use the Directional Gyro and the Artificial Horizon to get me safely out of the cloud.

To be honest I don't remember how I did it without getting into a graveyard spiral – but survive I did, otherwise you wouldn't be reading this fascinating tale.

You might think that was enough trouble for one trip. Not so.

Nearing Johannesburg I suddenly I found that there were a bunch of Harvards playing chicken with me. The first I noticed of this idiocy was when one came up vertically in front of me. I could clearly see the faces of the two morons who had their heads tilted back to look at me.

The aeroplane disappeared above me as it slowly became inverted. The bastards were doing a loop round me!

Then another Harvard swooped round ahead of me in a steep turn, and another came alongside and the crew started making impolite gestures at me. You would think they had better things to do with the taxpayers' money.

'I know how to sort you bastards out,' I thought. 'I will get right down on the deck – and then at least I will only have to look upwards to see you – you won't be able to attack me from underneath.'

What happened next took me completely by surprise. As I headed for ground level, three Harvards in formation came straight towards me from the right. They were also descending to ground level, and heading straight for me. I couldn't believe their idiot behaviour – this was getting bloody dangerous. Obviously the only thing for me to do was hold my heading and altitude – they would have to take evasive action, because legally I had the right of way. I continued staring at them in horror as they matched my descent to ground level.

What didn't click in my head was that they all had their undercarriages down.

Anyhow when I glanced ahead to see where I was going I found I was heading straight for a control tower.

I had flown slap over the four parallel runways at Donottar. The three aircraft that I thought were buzzing me were actually landing.

This was one of the few occasions in my life where my brain caught up with the situation. I turned right and climbed in the general direction of Lourenco Marques. Donottar would obviously notify Jan Smuts of my foolishness, and Smuts would have me on their radar. The last thing I wanted was for them to know was that I was going to Wonderboom. They would have a military reception committee waiting for me and would probably hurl me in a dungeon with spiders and rats.

I stayed at a couple of thousand feet – heading East – until I was quite sure Smuts had a good bearing on me, then I slowly descended below the radar and crept back to Wonderboom at 50 ft. Naturally all this took time.

As I taxied up to the hangar, there was the familiar figure of Zingi appearing out of the shadows. No sooner had the engine stopped than he opened the door and said. "Where the hell have you been, Davis?"

"I went to Durban like you told me, Skipper." I couldn't believe he would be that forgetful.

"Don't try to be smart with me, Davis. I was flying aeroplanes with guns on them when your pee-pee was the size of a shirt button." This was a favourite expression of his. Or sometimes he would tell me that he had more time inverted on the top of a loop, than I had in my entire log-book.

Actually I couldn't see what his flying hours had to do with his question about where I had come from, so I played dumb and just stared at him.

"Okay, let me put it another way. What time did you leave Durban? And don't lie to me, because I have already checked up."

I had no idea where this line of questioning was leading, so I told him it was 9.30.

"And the flight should take you three-and-a-half hours. So you should have been back here at one o'clock. What does your watch say now?"

"Just after one-thirty, Skipper."

"I see. So that extra half hour couldn't have taken you straight through the Military Flying Area at Donottar, and then on track for LM?"

"Hell no, Skipper."

"Good. That's what I told Smuts when they phoned."

"Thanks, Skipper."

He turned and headed back to his office.

I pushed the aeroplane into the hanger and crossed the seat-belts neatly over the seats. I was walking past Zingi's office with my little suitcase when he hailed me.

"Davis," he viewed me with the hint of a twisted smile. "It's lucky no one got your registration, isn't it?"

* * *

Windhoek

On the 17th of March, 1964, Zingi decided that a red Super Cub, ZS-DRS, which had been sitting mournfully in the back of the hangar for some months, suddenly needed to be in Windhoek.

He summonsed Bill Forftuin, a wild, mercenary character who spent much of his life in central Africa – flying for whichever side paid best. Bill's current mission was to convert me to the magic Super Cub. He either had great, unfounded, confidence in my abilities, or he was suffering from a hangover, because my logbook shows that my conversion lasted 20 minutes – two circuits. He thought that, together with the 140 hours already in my logbook, was all I needed to take the aircraft to Windhoek.

It did occur to me that Zingi and Bill had hatched a cunning plan to get rid of me. That was a pretty formidable trip in the days of no GPS no cell-phones, and pretty scratchy met forecasts. Also, in this case, no DI, no ADF and certainly no VOR. In fact, no nav-aids at all – apart from my maps, my watch and a compass.

Perhaps they hoped I would disappear into the desert and never be heard of again. And, of course, it would be a cash sale to the insurance company.

Anyhow I borrowed my wife's straw hat, because the aircraft had a Perspex panel in the roof; strapped a gallon can of water into the back seat and pointed her nose a bit south of west – towards my first refuelling point at Kuruman.

I am telling you this story, because what I remember most about it is the pure joy of basic navigation. I have always had a thing about maps, and there is no better way of appreciating one than to fly over the landscape and see how precisely it matches all the images on the chart. Every little kink in a river is faithfully reproduced on paper.

Also there is a certain satisfaction in holding the aircraft absolutely straight against a distant point, for a couple of minutes, and mentally averaging out the swings of the little compass. If it turned out that you were say 5 degrees off heading, then you would turn the aircraft a little and go through the procedure again. That's simply how we steered in the days when directional gyros were not part of our lives. They were costly, and heavy, optional extras that required vacuum pumps or drag-making venturi's.

For map-reading, my all-time favourite is the basic 1:1 000 000 World Aeronautical Chart (WAC). With us ordinary puddle-jumper pilots the only time you need more detail is if you are flying over densely populated areas, and if you need less detail, then you are probably flying some pressurised margarine-burner on an IF plan. And sitting above the clouds where you can't map-read in any case.

The leg to Kuruman was great fun. I kicked off at 6 o'clock in the morning and arrived there at 0910. In those days we only logged time in the air – not start-up to switch-off, as one does now.

There were plenty of features – little towns and big roads, then I crossed the railway line, between Lichtenburg and Colighy, at right angles, to get an accurate groundspeed check. The nav was very easy. Vryburg appeared on the nose.

Visibility was brilliant. I had left the Johannesburg smog belt, and I had the sun behind me, so all the buildings in the towns and villages sparkled with white walls like drive-in screens. There was no wind and the air was calm. From Vryburg, there is a dead straight road that takes you right in to Kuruman. I was finding this potentially scary nav to be a piece of cake, and huge fun.

My logbook shows that I was only on the ground for 20 minutes. That means 20 minutes from touch-down to takeoff. There were no formalities of any sort. It was like refuelling your car. I taxied up to the pumps. Did a pre-flight while the fuel was being pumped in, checked for water and took off again. Landing fees at small fields were unheard of.

When I set heading for Keetmanshoop, navigation took on a new cloak. You head out across a range of hills and then slap into the desert. The area is called Gordonia. There are no roads, railways, or villages. In fact if you found anything recognisable it would mean you were lost.

Actually there are tiny dots on the map that announce themselves as "Areas of Local Importance". They don't refer to things like the Voortrekker Monument, but perhaps to a mud puddle where goats like to drink. On rare occasions there might even be a couple of huts.

It is the same as flying over the sea, or above cloud. There is nothing, nothing, nothing to see. Actually that's not quite true. Because there are no magenta lines, your interest in what meagre topography there is, takes on a new level of importance. If you look carefully, you will notice that in desert areas on your map there are very faint little patches of minute dots that form little, slightly darker streaks.

I had always imagined that they were just the cartographer's artistic license. Sort of symbols to encourage the aerial navigator in the knowledge that he is indeed making progress across this featureless wasteland, almost like dragons and sea-monsters on old nautical charts.

Not so. I was amazed to find that they accurately indicate the lie of the sand dunes and that if you are crossing them at an angle which mirrors the smudges on your map, then you are indeed heading in the right direction. In fact they are accurate enough to serve as a check on your compass.

Oh, and there is one other set of features that can help the enthusiastic navigator. These are the pans which become more frequent after about half way. Unfortunately they all look pretty much the same. Sort of blotches that vary between a few hundred meters and a few miles across. Mostly they are not much use for navigation because they all look so similar. Occasionally you may get longish one that looks like maybe a crocodile, and you find yourself twiddling your map around to try and make the shape fit. Generally it is a waste of time.

You fly about 290(T) out of Kuruman and the landscape is about as featureless as the ocean – except there is one groundspeed check. About 20 miles into the flight you cross a railway line at right angles. I didn't have to allow for the climb because in the cool of the day there is little point in gaining much altitude. I considered that about 1000 ft AGL was more than high enough. Why climb – there is nothing to see and no one to talk to?

About two hours into the flight you cross a most extraordinary feature. It is the fence that demarks the border between South Africa and South West Africa, as it was known then.

The remarkable thing about this fence is that it runs exactly True North and True South in a dead straight line that disappears over both horizons. It is exactly on the 20 degree East line of longitude. This again gives you a good groundspeed check.

You may imagine that such a flight would be somewhat intimidating – and indeed it would if you were to ponder the consequences of an engine failure which dumped you in the desert. You would never be found, even if you had "overdue action" or Search and Rescue on your flight plan, because without an HF radio to keep you in touch with the real world, you were not allowed to file such a flight plan – international flight or not. So I had no flight-plan. Actually I don't think going to SWA was even considered an international flight in those days.

Anyway, baring mechanical nonsenses, or nasty winds, there was not much chance of getting lost. I simply adopted the old Francis Chichester trick of heading a few degrees off track and then picking up a line feature which leads you into your destination. In this case I turned a bit to the left of track, and when I reached the railway line I knew I would need to turn right to get to Keetmanshoop. It is a simple trick but it works like a strap.

While I was in Keetmans I did a 40 minute local flight. I can only think it was a demonstration for a prospective Super Cub buyer. Then I set sail for the dusty strip at Mariental.

I didn't need to navigate from a directional point of view – I simply followed the railway line which runs roughly due north. It is only 120 nautics to Mariental, and is pretty much half way to Windhoek. But groundspeed is everything. By now I had a healthy Northerly wind which got stronger the further North I flew. With no wind I could easily have made Windhoek direct, with fuel to spare. As it turned out the Mariental fuel stop was a life-saver.

Again, refuelling was a speedy business and I was off on my final leg to Eros, just outside Windhoek, where I touched down at 4:15 in the afternoon.

That meant that I had been sitting in that cramped little aeroplane for 10 hrs and 15 minutes that day. I have never, before or since, logged that many hours in a single 24 hour period. I am sure it wasn't legal, and I have to admit to feeling fairly stuffed by the end of the day.

That night, I was at the "Safari", a famous pilots' wateringhole, getting stuck into a well-deserved steak when I heard the folks at the next table talking about a subject that has always fascinated me – ballooning.

After a bit I couldn't resist asking if I could join them to learn more. Soon, with the alcohol flowing amongst us, they asked me if I would like to go for an early morning flight with them. Naturally I was ecstatic. I would be there before dawn pulling ropes and carrying heavy things and doing whatever was necessary to repay their kindness.

As the evening wore on, their stories became filled with bravado and machoness. I realised I had let myself in for a flight with a bunch of cowboys who would still be well over the limit by the time they lit their burners in the morning.

I invented a previously forgotten early-morning appointment, and bid them goodnight.

I returned to headquarters the next day on the SAA, milk-run, DC4 Skymaster. It had to be one of the most impressive flights of my life. I wheedled my way into the cockpit, and captain decided that as it was such a nice smooth day we would fly the first leg, to Keetmans, below ground level, in the Fish River Canyon.

This was an unbelievable flight apart from the impressiveness of the canyon, which is a half-scale Grand Canyon, there was the flying. The canyon has some fairly sharp corners in it, which meant throwing our four-engined mount on to its wingtip and hauling on the pole. I have no idea how the passengers enjoyed the G forces, but we had no official complaints.

Years later, I was training students on the Border during the Bush War, and I remembered this flight, so each student had to do that subterranean leg as part of their cross-country navigation flight.

On one such flight I remember, while banking round one of the bends in the canyon, suddenly having this vision of the four massive props of a DC4 Skymaster thundering straight towards us as the captain stood it on its ear while rounding the corner from the other side.

Anyhow when I got back to headquarters in the afternoon, Zingi enquired whether I knew anything of the balloon that had pranged in Windhoek.

It was the same guys – I think there were four of them – and they had managed to become entangled with power lines and had all been killed in a mass of flames.

Moral? Listen to that little voice.

While this story is largely about featureless nav I must finish off by telling you a story about what getting lost *really* means.

During the war when Old Piet, who was probably in his early 20s then, was flying a Miles Magister, from Bloem to Cape Town. He was above cloud with little idea of where he was, so he did the unforgivable thing of letting down on ETA.

Imagine his surprise when he broke cloud, there was no Cape Town. In fact there was nothing to be seen – except the sea.

It stretched from horizon to horizon in all directions. Either the upper winds had been a lot stronger than he expected, or his compass had curled up its toes. He had no idea whether he was off the South coast or the West coast, so it was not easy to guess where Africa, might be hiding.

His situation was made worse because he was beginning to run short of fuel.

Piet headed in a general North-Easterly direction and hoped for the best. It turned out to be his lucky day because he soon spotted a smudge of black smoke on the horizon, and this slowly turned into a convoy of ships.

Naturally, he was overjoyed. He wrote a note, explaining his predicament, on the back of one of his charts, flew low over the lead ship and dropped the map, intending it to land on the deck so they could send out a boat to collect him when he ditched – his fuel state was desperate by this time.

Piet's note missed the mark, so he dropped another, which also fell in the water. His final map did no better, but the ship stopped and put out a lifeboat. Piet ditched, swam a short distance and was hauled aboard.

No sooner was he on the ship than they dragged him up to the captain, still dripping wet. It turned out the skipper was a man of few words. "What's your message?" He demanded.

"Message?" Piet replied.

"Convoys don't stop to pull second lieutenants out of the sea. I assume you have a message of vital importance to the war effort."

"In that case it's just as well you didn't get my charts." Piet replied. "I was asking you to stop and rescue me – I was lost and almost out of fuel."

It was indeed Piet's lucky day.

But he said that, for the rest of the trip, he was treated like that commodity that has a reputation for sticking to army blankets.

* * *

If you enjoyed these stories, check out Jim's second book in this series.

* * *

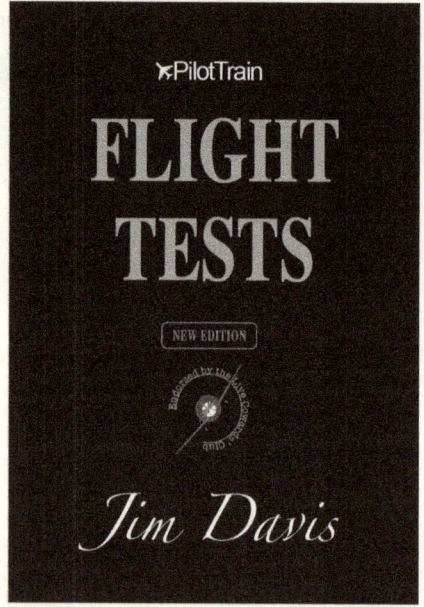

www.ingramcontent.com/pod-product-compliance
Lightning Source LLC
Chambersburg PA
CBHW032000080426
42735CB00007B/454